AF428712

# UNLOCKING ORAL FUNCTION:

## Understanding And Managing The Shortened Dental Arch

Dr Peter S

# ACKNOWLEDGEMENT

*I wish to acknowledge my appreciation to certain people.*

*First and foremost, I would like to thank **THE ALMIGHTY** for his blessing, who have led me so far and continues to lead me in the journey of life.*

*My heart filled thanks to **Mrs. JOSEPHINE MARY S (Mummy), Mr. SELVAM SAVARIAPPAN (Appa)**, my sister **Miss ROSY S** for the constant love, support and encouragement they've rendered me with.*

*I consider it a privilege and honor to thank my HOD Professor & Head of Department of Prosthodontics, Crown and Bridge & Implantology,            **Dr PRASAD ARAVIND** for his unlimited help, support, and sound advice through this post graduate journey.*

*With great pleasure, I acknowledge my guide **Dr ABHINAV MOHAN** Reader, for his expertise and advice throughout the completion of my work.*

*I am also deeply indebted to **Dr DIPIN PP, Dr LINO PAUL, Dr UNNI, Dr AHANAF ABDULLA, Dr NIROSHA, Dr ANKITHA, Dr CIMMY** Senior lecturers, for their very valuable comments. They have raised many precious points and I hope that I have managed to address several of them.*

*I feel incredibly honored to work under the supervision and guidance of all of them.*

*I am grateful to my beloved seniors **Dr RAGUL I, Dr JOBIN JOY, Dr PREMKUMAR, Dr SREYA MAHESH** and my fellow juniors **Dr SHABANA & Dr JAILAAN MURSHITHA** for generously sharing their valuable thoughts and ideas.*

*I would like to extend my special thanks to, **Dr HARISHINI S (Hulk) and Dr PUSHPASANTHY (Push)**, for their invaluable help and unwavering support throughout this journey.*

*I will never forget my boys **RAGUUL, RHOSE and JERIE** who have been there for me in every situation of my life, and I hope our bond lasts forever....also with my girls **SWATHI CHECHI, THEE AND SULU.***

*I like to extend my thanks to my people **Roz, San, Pooja, Bishnu, Athu Zia, Drish, Misha and Follee** and everyone.*

*I want to express my heartfelt thanks to everyone who stood by me during my toughest times. I proudly acknowledge that this journey would not have been possible without their unwavering support.*

**Dr. Peter S**

# WORDS THAT GAVE ME HOPE...

**Use your smile to change the world, don't let the world change your smile.**

\- Dr. Ashwini Elangovan (To me)

**Hakuna Matata**

# MUSIC HEALS...

# CONTENTS

# SHORTENED DENTAL ARCH

## INTRODUCTION

Clinicians may hold the belief that all the missing teeth should be replaced to ensure a satisfactory oral function and a healthy masticatory system, as the loss of molar support may lead to temporomandibular joint dysfunction, occlusal instability and impairment of mastication.[1,2] However, the hypothesis that tooth loss will result in sub-optimal oral function and comfort has often been questioned. [3] Some posterior teeth may be important to the aesthetics of the smile and there may be other emotional factors associated with tooth loss. While maximum patients seek the prosthetic replacement of the anterior teeth more as compare to posterior teeth, [1] replacement of a missing premolar may also be requested for aesthetic purpose. In many cases, the cost and the actual need for the restoration of the complete dental arch should be carefully considered.[4]

Another common concept is that missing teeth should be replaced to prevent the potential detrimental effects on the dentition. [5] However, there is a substantial difference between the professional's assessment and the patient's perception of need for prosthetic rehabilitation.[6] Patients adapt to a new dental condition and they may be satisfied with less than 28 teeth.[7]

Aesthetics appears to be the main reason for prosthetic treatment in general and patients with missing anterior teeth are less satisfied with their oral condition and have higher perceived need to replace the missing anterior teeth.[8] However, not all patients with missing anterior teeth will seek prosthetic treatment and financial constraints are the most common reason for non- replacement of the missing teeth. [9]

In 1981 the concept of the 'shortened dental arch' was proposed by Kayser. [10] Clinical studies conducted by Kayser and his colleagues, concluded that for sufficient masticatory function and a healthy occlusion, four occlusal units are needed. One occlusal unit has been defined as one pair of occluding premolars and one pair of occluding molars are considered to be two occlusal units. The shortened dental arch (SDA) can be defined as the type of dentition with reduced or even absence of the molars and/or premolars.[4,11] However, a frequent application is for a compromised dentition absent of all the molar teeth.

In 1992, the World Health Organization stated that a functional and aesthetic dentition requires no less than 20 well distributed teeth. [12]

# SHORTENED DENTAL ARCH AND MASTICATORY FUNCTION

A successful course of treatment depends on the patient adapting to alteration in arch length brought on by gradual tooth loss, even if masticatory efficacy and aptitude are important elements in oral functionality. Oral functionality depends on the patient's capacity to adjust to changes in dental arch length brought on by tooth loss. Masticatory efficiency and masticatory ability are two crucial aspects of it. Subjective and objective assessments can be utilized to classify the literature on masticatory efficiency and ability during the past 50 to 60 years Interviews with patients who are assessing their own masticatory functionality are typically used to assess subjective masticatory function or masticatory competence. Measuring the patient's capacity to grind food is a standard part of an objective examination of masticatory function or efficiency. Overall, the body of research shows that masticatory function is decreased when there are fewer than 20 teeth that are uniformly distributed across the mouth. Rarely is the relationship between the length of the tooth arch and masticatory effectiveness discussed in the literature. In a study, 118 patients were divided into 6 groups according to the length and symmetry of the shortened dental arch in a cross-sectional clinical investigation [8]. There were two patterns seen of change in oral function, the dentition had been reduced to 4 occlusal units in 1 group, masticatory efficiency altered gradually? Thereafter, it declined quickly.Masticatory efficiency gradually improved at a nearly consistent rate in the second group. The authors hypothesised that as long as at least 4 occlusal units—which must be symmetrically positioned—remain, patients have the adaptive capacity to retain acceptable oral function in shorter dental arches. Another study compared patient evaluations of masticatory effectiveness in 54 individuals with complete dentitions with those from 43 people with SDAs. The findings showed that although SDA patients' masticatory function, food perception, food consumption was all impacted, the patients experienced a reduction that was acceptable [10]. In a different study, the oral functionalityof patients with shorter dental arches was contrasted with that of individuals who had detachable partial dentures that extended their dental arches distally [11]. The overall functionality of patient's wearing RPD's and FPD's showed similar results. Overall, the study's findings revealed that distal extension RPDs did not enhance oral functionality for SDA patients, and the majority of concerns seemed to be about aesthetics because of anterior tooth loss. A recent study compared the masticatory skills of people with full dental arches to those subjects with shorter dental arches in Tanzania. The SDA patients varied in arch length and arch symmetry and had 0 to 8 pairs of occluding posterior teeth. Masticatory capacity was evaluated based on 20 typical Tanzanian dishes' perceived mastication challenges. Patients with very short arches—0 to 2 pairs of teeth, including premolars—had the highest rates of complaints and the most challenging mastication. Forparticipants with undamaged premolar regions and at least one set of occluding molars,the prevalence of complaints was only 3% to 5%. Other subject groups, those who had a variable number of premolars and molars, reported a middle-sized number of complaints (33 percent to 54 percent). According to the study, there is a negative correlation between the perceived difficulty of mastication and the number of pairs of occluding teeth. For instance, patients with 0 to 2 pairs of occluding premolars had very poor masticatory skills. Similarly, those with asymmetric dental arches and irregular tooth distribution reported more difficult mastication than individuals with more full dental arches. Harder foods made any discrepancies in masticatory skills worse. Overall, the authors came tothe conclusion that an SDA does not reduce masticatory efficiency if the premolar areas are intact and there is at least one pair of occluding molars. And when a patient has fewer occluding premolars and/or asymmetrical arches, there is a considerable impairment of masticatory function, especially with hard food. However, according to some writers, SDAs do not cause changes in food preferences even when patients only have the adequate masticatory ability when 20 or more "well distributed" teeth—that is, when anterior and premolar teeth are still present— remain [12]. Therefore, reduced masticatory function and related alterations or shifts in food preferences only become apparent when there are fewer than 10 pairs of occluding teeth. 12 factors relating to prosthetics, Occlusal stability, creating the proper vertical dimension, and maintaining the health of the soft and hard tissues as well as that of the temporomandibular joint are all prosthodontic factors in patient care. A better definition of occlusal stability may be the stability of tooth positioning relative to its spatial relationship in the occluding dental arches. Occlusal stability is sometimes defined as the absence of the tendency for teeth to migrate other than the normal physiologic compensatory movements that occur over time [13,14]. Periodontal stability, number of teeth in arch interdental distance, occlusal contacts, and tooth wear are some of the factors which affect occlusal stability. When one or more teeth from an arch are missing, there is frequently tooth mobility, tooth migration, and supra-eruption of opposing teeth. In SDAs, grinding of distal tooth may lead to upsurge of anterior load, which in turn increases the frequency and intensity of SDAs and interdental spacing. In SDAs, distal tooth migrating might lead to an increased anterior load, which in turn raises the quantity and severity of anterior occlusal contacts as well as interdental space [15]. When unopposed teeth and single-standing teeth lack proper periodontal support, these consequences may be exaggerated. Similar to how tooth movement can alter the vertical and horizontal overlap, occlusal wear, and posterior support loss, among other things. Few researchers have examined the relationship between shorter dental arches and occlusal stability, despite the fact that it is commonly accepted that alterations in occlusal balance led to tooth movement, migration, and supra-eruption. Extremely small dental arches, particularly those with only 0 to 2 pairs of occluding teeth in premolar region, are thought to diminish occlusal stability. While longer dental arches those with three to four occluding units are said to have stronger occlusal stability, elderlypatients typically experience more occlusal integrity changes [16]. SDAs made up of anterior and premolar teeth meet oral functional demands and show patterns of vertical overlap and occlusal tooth wear that are analogous to those seen in full dental arches [17]. Although patients with SDAs have more anterior teeth in occlusal contact, more interdental spacing and lower alveolar bone scores (i.e., the height of the alveolar bone at the distal surface of each premolar) than patients with complete or longer dental arches, these differences in dentition and occlusal characteristics appear to remain stable over time. This shows that long-term occlusal stability is, in fact, a feature of the SDA. There aren't many data available on the frequency of TMJ issues in people with reduced dental arches. In a study, people with SDA and controls with entire dental arches were comparedto SDA subjects with an intact anterior region and 0 to 8 posteriorly occlusive pairs of teeth. According to the study, participants with only one lateral posterior support and those without any posterior support experienced a higher prevalence of joint clicking/ crepitation. However, there were no differences between the SDA and control groups in terms of discomfort, mandibular mobility, maximal mouth opening, or clicking/ crepitation of the joints. However, it was discovered that diminished posterior supportwas substantially associated with increased tooth wear. Even though there is no proof that TMJ issues are caused by SDA, it was observed that when either unilaterally or bilaterallylacking posterior support, there is increased risk for pain and joint noises [18]. It was depicted by another study that there is a possibility that SDAs could overload the TMJand teeth, which could lead to TMD and periodontal disease. A FEM (fine element) model was used to quantify the occlusal forces and joint loads from electromyographic masticatory muscle investigations [19], and the calculated values were then compared to the actual measured occlusal forces. At all times, the occlusal force per root surface area was maximum on the most posterior tooth, the joint loads seemed to be declining overall even if the occlusal force on each individual tooth increased with missing molar occlusion. There were no signs that an SDA might overload the TMJ or the teeth,indicating that neuromuscular regulatory systems possess potential of efficiently regulating the maximum clenching force under a range of occlusal settings. Customer comfort dentures need functional and emotional adaptation from patients, and some may never succeed. Therefore, a patient may be unsatisfied and occasionally intolerable of a denture based on subjective evaluation of comfort, functionality, and appearance, even when the placed prosthesis may satisfy all subjective criteria regarding fit, quality, and aesthetics. The correlation between dentist and patient opinions of dentures typically isn't great since patient evaluation criteria are hard to quantify [20]. During the treatment ofSDA patient, these incongruities between clinician and patient perception are crucial. Fewclinical investigations have evaluated patient oral comfort objectively, which is commonly measured by the absence of pain or distress, masticatory capacity, and dental appearance in terms of arch length. There were no discernible variations in pain or discomfort between the three groups when the oral comfort of SDA patients was compared to that of SDAs and distal ex tension RPDs and for subjects with complete dental arches, and only 8% of the SDA participants reported reduced masticatory function. RPDs were reported to be unsatisfactory by 20% of SDA and RPD patients, and many patients discontinued using them for longer periods of time. There were no signs that offering distal extension RPDs improved oral comfort for SDA patients, even though an SDA can marginally reduce patient satisfaction with their mouths [21]. Another study using patient questionnaires discovered that even while patients' masticatory function was enhanced when bilateral RPDs were used to correct shortened mandibles, they not only preferred not to wear them but also there were signs of negative effects on the remaining teeth. Patients who received distal cantilever resin-bonded FPDs to correct the reduced mandibular dental arch reported improved overall satisfaction and better mammillary ability than those who received RPDs[22]. Clinical evaluation of SDAs various individuals having shortened dental arches receive treatment, but the SDA is not officially recognizedas a part of clinical care, and there are not many publications in the literature that discuss clinical attitudes about the SDA in current treatments. The SDA is broadly acknowledged but not commonly used in the UK, according to a survey administered by British writers [23]. Regarding patient oral function, comfort, and wellbeing, the results of SDA therapy (SDAT) were discovered to be acceptable in about 82 percent of patients. Approximately 88% of people who participated in survey said they had prescribed SDAT in the previous five years, however only 37% said they had to lengthen the reduced dental arches after taking SDAT. The 64 restorative dentistry faculty members at the Nijmegen School of Dentistry in the Netherlands were the subject of a second questionnaire-based study that evaluated their views and use of the SDA concept in clinical practise [24]. There was a response rate of 64%, and all respondents all except one thought the small dental arch concept had a place in clinical practise. Considerations of oral functionality, prosthodontic treatment, and patient comfort become more significant as the number of surviving teeth declines [25,26]. Even though restoration of the entire dental arch, that is, upto and including the second molars, is ideal, not every patient will be able to have this course of treatment due to practical or economic reasons. For vulnerable and high-risk patients such as those who are immunocompromised and undergoing radiotherapy, chemotherapy, or both, complete dental arch restoration may also not be advised, however, the issue of what constitutes an appropriate and reasonable level of care for the partially dentate patient still needs to be addressed, with the apparent corollary of whetherthe

expense of care is reasonable given the expected and/or actual clinical outcome [27]. A

functional, aesthetically pleasing, natural dentition of at least 20 teeth that does notrequire

the use of prosthetics is what constitutes acceptable oral health throughout life. This suggests

that adult patients have appropriate oral functionality if their second premolars are posterior

most teeth in the arch. This problem is addressed by the idea ofthe shorter but still

functioning dental arch (SDA), which, according to the literature, hasa number of advantages

over conventional occlusion theories [28]. The SDA protocol, in particular, places less focus

on restorative procedures for the back of the mouth. In other words, the SDA might provide

high-quality care at a low cost without running the danger of treating the patient excessively

[29]. The second premolar region is when the occlusal platform is terminated by the SDAT

protocol. As there are no posterior implants required,the surgical implant placement and

restoration processes are made simpler, which may be advantageous for the implant patient

[30]. The SDA protocol may also be advantageous forhigh-risk patients since it shortens the

treatment schedule without sacrificing oral functionality by restraining the dental arch length.

In many studies, it has been determined that the loss of teeth is related with reduced

masticatory performance and few of these studies were reviewed. The number of teeth and,

in particular, the number of the occluding pairs have been found to be crucial for the

masticatory performance. This may be explained by the reduction in teeth reducing the

occlusal surface area and decreasing the maximum bite force. The loss of the posterior teeth

may decrease the capacity to break down food and it can reduce the chewing efficiency by

50%. Subjects with SDA carry out 70% more chewing cycles. [16,17] In addition, the reduced

dentition can be related to insufficient nutritional intake in vitamins and fibres with adverse

effects on the health status with a preference for more soft food and confectionaries than vegetables. Krall *et al.* [15] found that impairment dentition is related with insufficient nutrient intake with adverse effects on health status, while others report that chewing efficiency and the nutritional intake in vitamins and fibres is relatedto the number of posterior teeth and others that the masticatory performance is related to the number of the remaining teeth. Fueki *et al.* [18] found that the reduction of the occlusal platform may reduce the bite force and Kreulen *et al.* [16] demonstrated that subjects with SDA have 50% less chewing efficiency.

There is a significant influence of the position of the remaining teeth and the number of the occlusal contacts on the masticatory performance and are more critical for the chewing performance than the actual number of remaining teeth. Missing molars with bounded spaces are more obvious to a patient than a free end saddle and can be the reasonbehind chewing discomfort. [27] The loss of molars have a limited impact and it can be compensated by larger food particles for swallowing and larger number of chewing cyclesbefore swallowing.

The SDA as a treatment modality has been considered to be successful when 20 well distributed teeth are present. Research by Kayser [10] demonstrated that the masticatory function may be reduced when the occlusal units are less than four in a symmetrical position or less than six in asymmetrical position and others have confirmed that the number of the occlusal contacts are more important than the number of teeth for the chewing performance. Subjects with 20 well established teeth can adapt to the gradualloss of teeth, can eat almost all types of food and are satisfied with their masticatory function. [25]

# SHORTENED DENTAL ARCH AND
# TEMPOROMANDIBULAR JOINT

Despite various researches, there is no clear causal association between the SDA and temporomandibular joint dysfunction (TMD) although tooth extraction itself can be a factor in causing trauma to the TMJ. The loss of the posterior teeth has been shown to predispose the dysfunction of the temporomandibular joints[31] as well as cause histologicalchanges within the joint, displacement of the disc, degenerative changes as well asaccelerate the development of existing pathology and TMD. [30]

On the contrary, a small number of studies have concluded that the SDA does notprovoke any mandibular dysfunction[31,32] as the stomatognathic system and the TMJs canadapt to changes of the dentition. Loss of posterior teeth is not correlated with TMJ overloading as the neuromuscular regulatory mechanism prevents this.[33] Studies showed that SDA can result in increased tooth grinding or clenching habits [31] but TMD was mildor infrequent there were no signs and symptoms of cranio-mandibular joint dysfunction. Others have shown that unilateral loss of posterior teeth does not produceany intra articular pathological changes and it can aggravate only existing pathology of the temporomandibular joint.[34] Therefore, there continues to be evidence for and against the effect of the SDA on the multifactorial TMJ conditions including TMD.

# SHORTENED DENTAL ARCH AND OCCLUSAL STABILITY

Various studies have focused on the occlusal stability of the SDA as tooth migration is a recognized feature in incomplete dentitions. Subsequently, the loss of the teeth and tooth movement may lead to changes in the occlusal contacts, the interdental spacing and the alveolar bone support although these changes are usually negligible and remain stable over time. Therefore, they have been defined as more adaptive as compare to pathologicaland result in a new equilibrium. [35] Other studies report that the spacing may increase andbe unstable and can have a negative impact on existing periodontal disease. [36] Several studies demonstrated that tooth loss does not increase tooth wear, and subjects with SDA often have increased interdental spacing but it does not necessarily indicate a pathologicalcondition as these changes are adaptive character.

# SHORTENED DENTAL ARCH AND PROSTHETIC REHABILITATION

The presence of one occluding pair of molars and an intact premolar region or 20 well distributed teeth seems to be sufficient for chewing function [37] although this may be due to longer chewing periods. The bilateral or unilateral free end removable partial denture does not improve the masticatory function and the patient's satisfaction or provide oral comfort; a denture may also have adverse effects on the soft and hard tissues whereas the SDA may be preserved for over 27 years. [38] However, the free end removable partial denture maybe be favourable in cases of extreme shortened dental arch where the oral function has been severely impaired. [37,39]

The resin bonded bridge may be an important tool in tooth replacement in some clinical cases and has been shown to result in less accumulation of plaque, better oral comfort andmore patient satisfaction compare to removable partial denture in many clinical situations which may be applicable to the SDA.

A popular alternative option to the SDA is dental implant. They are a more conservative long-term option as compare to long span bridges, with the additional advantage of preserving bone and providing better posterior support than dentures. [35] However, a UK study of 140 cases of SDA in the UK revealed that 67% were restored with a chrome framed RPD, 26% with an acrylic RPD, and only 6% restored with an implant restoration and 1% with RBBs. [40] Current trends show an increasing in popularity in the use of dental implants for many reasons but it is recognised that many factors need to be considered and taken into account. [41] There are many systems available but few guidelines for clinicians.[42]

The Dutch prosthodontist Arnd Käyser in 1981 first used the term _shortened dental arches' (SDAs) to describe a dentition in which most posterior teeth are missing. This condition is frequently seen where posterior teeth are lost due to dental caries and periodontal disease, whereas anteriors and premolars tend to survive longer. The resultsof clinical studies by Käyser et al.[1,3] showed there is sufficient adaptive capacity in people with a SDA when at least four occlusal units remain, and this capacity starts to diminish after having less than four occlusal units (one unit corresponds to a pair of occluding premolars). SDA can also be defined as a dentition with an intact anterior region and a reduction of occluding posterior pairs, which starts posteriorly, as molars are more prone to be lost. Edentulism was regarded as a normal characteristic of aging in the past, but the use of current disease prevention techniques along with advances in restorative dentistry have created the opportunity for the dentition to be maintainedthroughout old age which is a favourable trend since the percentage of elderly people is increasing.[4,7] For many patients and clinicians the preservation of complete dental arches(28 teeth) has been a traditional ideal primary goal, but for the majority of elderly patients, this is not possible, therefore, is no longer considered a goal in a contemporary approach to restorative dentistry. In 1992, the World Health Organization stated the aim of treatment to achieve oral health is the retention, throughout life, of a functional,esthetic, natural dentition of not less than twenty teeth and not requiring alternative to a prosthesis. The exact number of teeth needed to satisfy functional demands was not determined as these demands are different between individuals. [5] However, failure to replace posterior teeth may result in adverse effects such as insufficient chewing ability, temporomandibular joint disorder (TMD), tooth migration, and over-eruption. [(6,9)7,8] Furthermore, following tooth loss patients may experience discomfort, lack of a satisfying appearance, difficulty chewing, a loss of appetite, and stress. Keeping a natural, healthy, and functional dentition for life has a positive effect on the quality of life. Therefore, the restoration or placement of prostheses should be able to meet the patient's needs in addition to being functionally sufficient. [(9)] It appears the current goals of dental care is the maintenance of natural dentition with regard to social and biological factors such as esthetic, speech, chewing, and oral comfort. [(43)] Alveolar bone resorption tends to affect the mandible more than the maxilla most probably due to the narrow denture bearing area with less favourable distribution of the occlusal load. [(8)] A functionally oriented therapeutic approach has been introduced for patients with reduced dentition becausebone loss is more extensive on the labial aspect of the anterior region of the ridge, more equal on the buccal and lingual aspects of the ridge in the premolar region, and the loss is greater on the lingual aspect of the ridge in the molar region. A dental arch can be extended to obtain a functional level with one of the following options: [(7)] • Removable partial denture (RPD) • Cantilever bridges • Overdentures. The traditional prosthodontic treatment of the partially edentulous jaw or SDA tended to be the removable partial denture (RPD) to substitute the missing teeth for optimum function and aesthetics. 1 The RPD has been regarded as a predictable treatment option, but it can cause the breakdown of periodontal tissue supporting the remaining teeth and bone resorption underneath the denture base. [(3)] Recent therapeutic options in the treatment of SDA have been suggested: 1 • Replacement with a fixed restoration to the second premolar • The use of implants in combination with a fixed partial denture Several factors in the restoration of a SDA clinical scenario were tested by Witter et al. [(11,12)] including: • Masticatory ability • Occlusal factors •

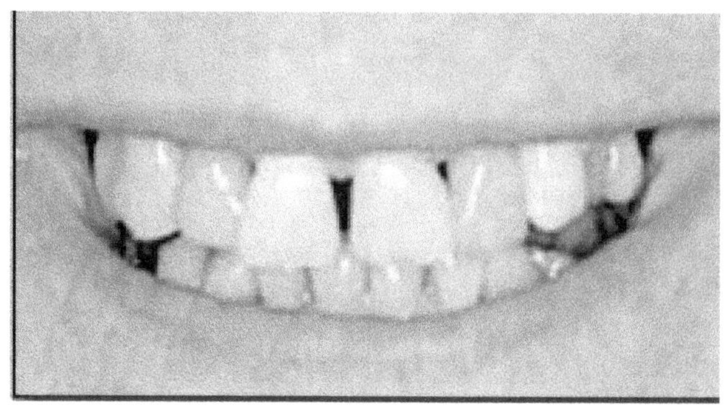

Fig.1 Compromised smile

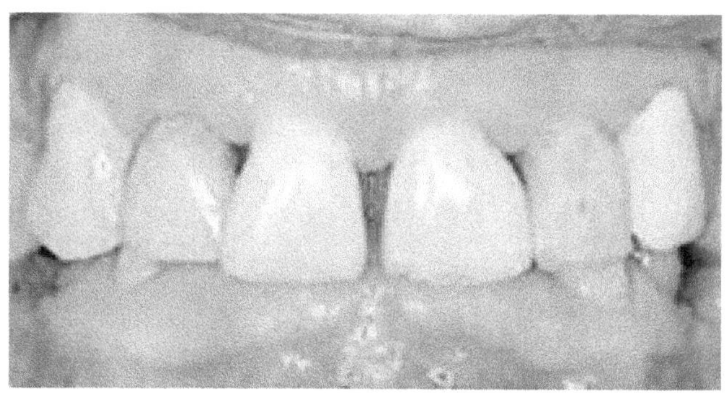

Fig Presence of a deep overbite

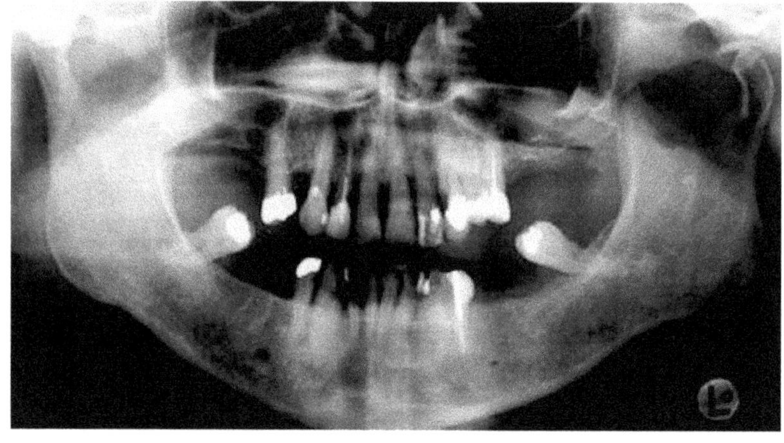

Fig.3 Panoramic radiograph showing

horizontal bone loss and tilting ofmolars

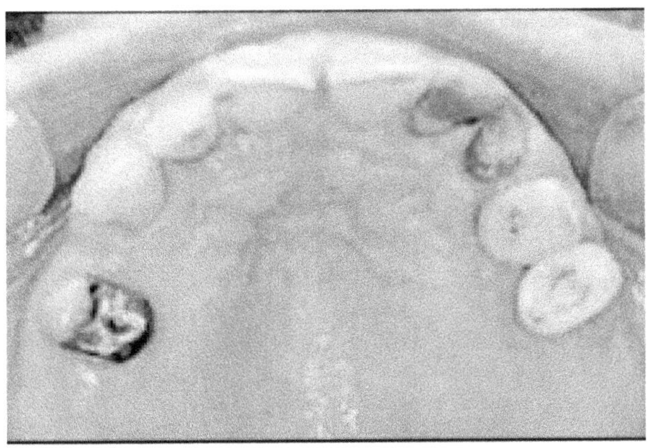

Fig.4 Occlusal view of the maxillary dentition after periodontal therapy

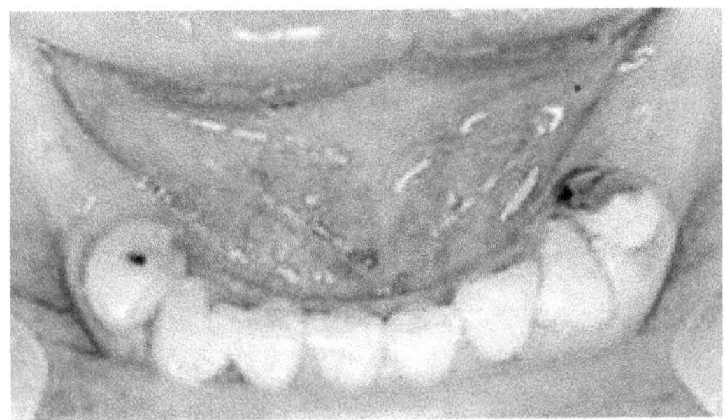

Fig.5 Occlusal view of the mandibular dentition after periodontal therapy

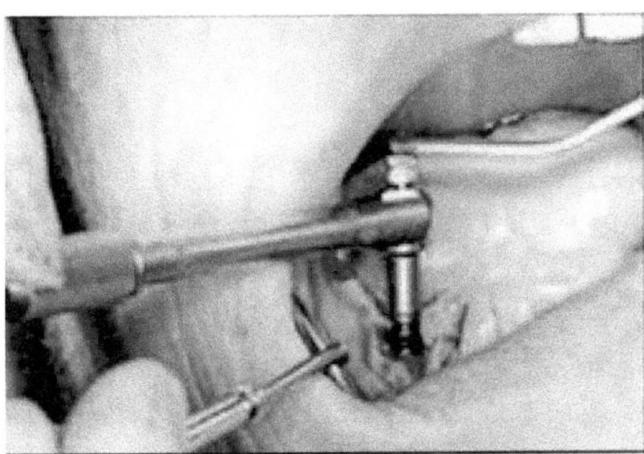

Fig.6 Surgical phase of implant placement

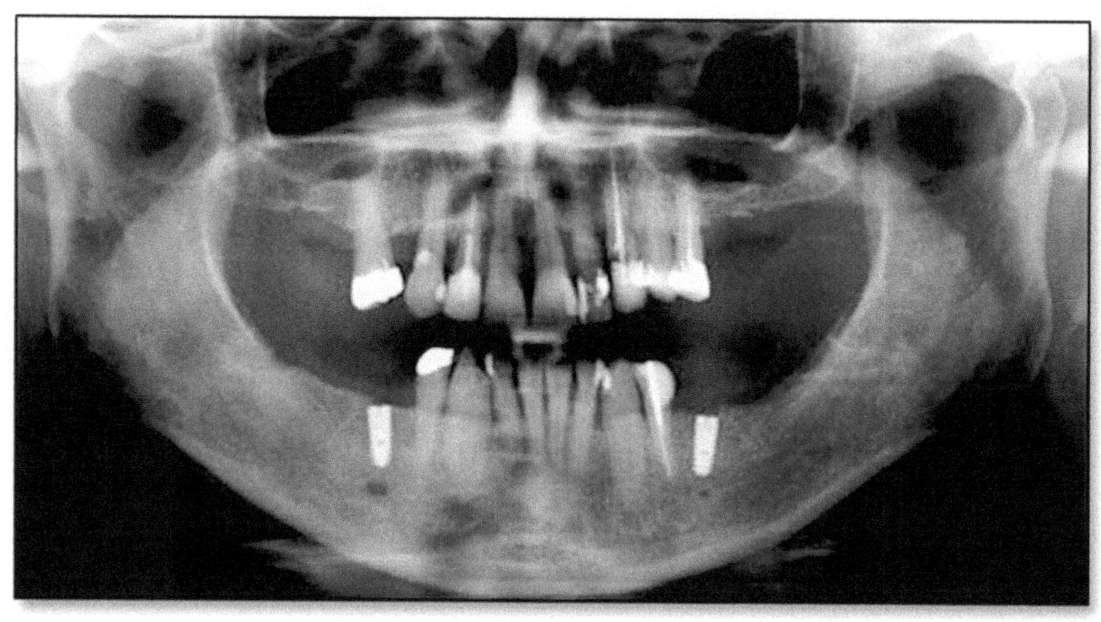

Fig.7 A panoramic radiographic image showing the implant placed

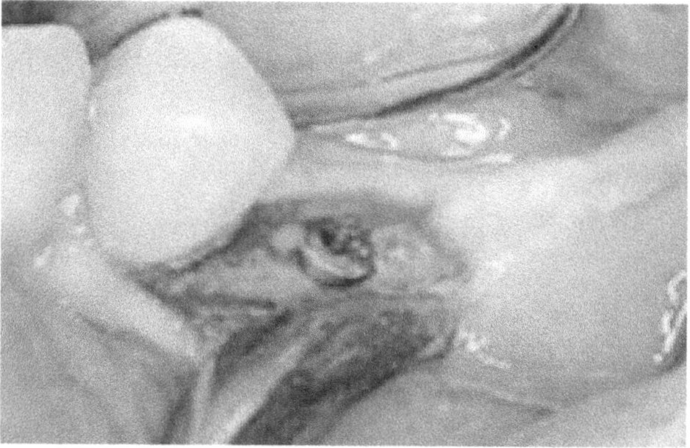

Fig.8 At the second stage surgery, bone was found to have grown above the

implant

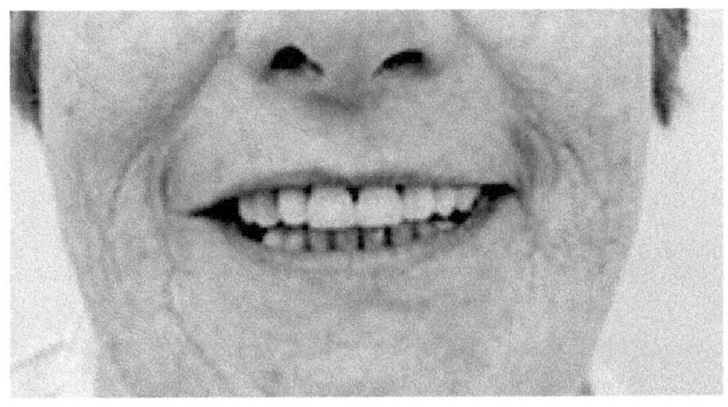

Fig.9 Final restoration were inserted and the bite was opened

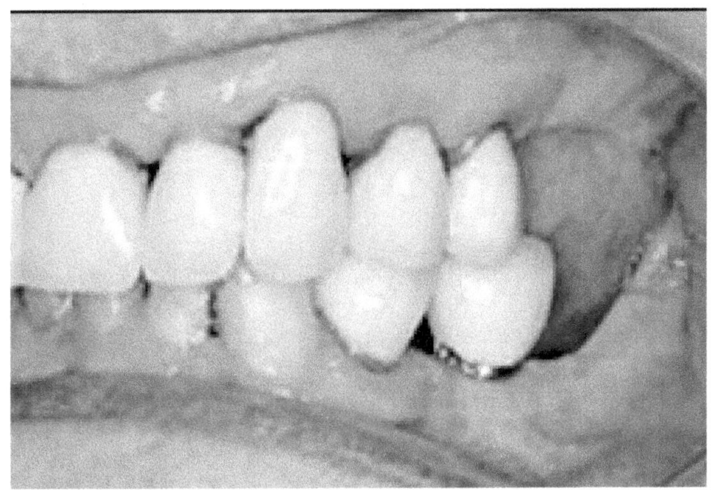

Fig.10 On a six- m o n t h recall visit he patient
reported comfort regarding
chewing and appearance, and oral health was satisfactory

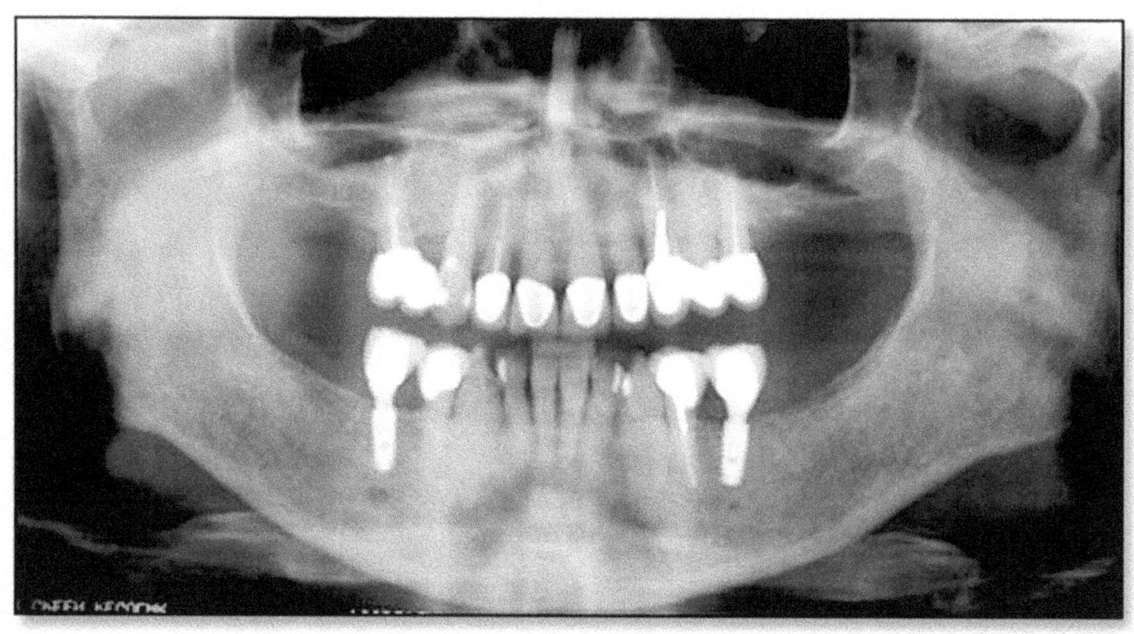

Fig.11 A panoramic radiograph taken at the six months recall visit.

# SHORTENED DENTAL ARCH AND DENTISTS' ATTITUDES

Only a limited number of studies have tried to evaluate dentists' attitudes towards the SDA concept although it has been widely accepted and has an important place in contemporary dentistry. [11]58 While many dentists consider the chewing function, aesthetics and oral comfort in SDA to be satisfactory, the concept is not widely implemented and the majority of the dentists tend to rehabilitate the SDA with removable partial dentures. [44]57

## Clinical considerations

While considering the prosthetic rehabilitation of patients, all the advantages and risks of any treatment options should carefully be evaluated as there are various options including fixed and removable prosthesis, using implants, and adhesive dentistry; however, any prosthetic treatment incurs a biological price. [45]

The minimally invasive resin bonded bridge, may be considered reversible, inexpensive, where clinically possible, not time consuming and patients may easily adapt toit. Implants, which can lead to unpredictable soft tissues aesthetics, remain the most expensive treatment option. [12] The removable partial denture is a non-invasive and low- cost treatment option for the prosthetic rehabilitation of patients with compromised dentition. It may be an excellent method for the replacement of the posterior teeth and missing soft and hard tissues although creates an increased risk of caries and periodontal breakdown, although adequate oral and denture hygiene with regular recall appointments will decrease the damage on the remaining teeth and the periodontal tissues. [12]

Based on their six years follow up study of patients with SDA they reported the following:

- Minor changes occurred with respect to occlusal contact, overbite, interdental spacing, and alveolar bone support in both the SDA group and a SDA group with an RPD. The SDA clinical scenario provided durable occlusal stability even though theywere left untreated.

- This study revealed SDA patients had sufficient mandibular stability to prevent signs and symptoms of TMD syndrome, so a SDA alone was not a risk factor for developing TMD.

- SDA provided sufficient oral comfort in terms of chewing ability and appearance compared with using RPD's.

- Oral function was not improved in the SDA scenario with the use of removable partial denture RPD.

- The patients experienced satisfaction regarding their oral function.

- It was also concluded the SDA clinical scenario has a useful effect on clinicalpractice and should be considered as a treatment option.

In a long-term nine-year follow-up study the SDA clinical scenario did not result in occlusal collapse. [13] The occlusal changes in a SDA were self-limiting and adaptive, leading to a new equilibrium and so extending the SDA by prosthetic devices was not necessary to prevent occlusal collapse. Also, no statistically significant differences were detected between restoration with an RPD or not to an SDA scenario in a randomized multi-centre study. Within both treatment options, an improvement of Oral Health Qualityof Life index was achieved. Out of these studies it was concluded SDA can maintain oral functions, prevent temporomandibular joint (TMJ) dysfunction, and provide long-term occlusal stability even when compared with complete dental arches. Although the restoration of a SDA has a sound biomechanical rationale it requires conditions such as healthy supporting tissues of the remaining teeth, and no parafunctional habits such as heavy bruxism. [3,46] There was, however, a discrepancy between the theoretical and practical acceptance of the restoration of SDA among dentists in many countries in that the option was widely accepted

# PROBLEMS AND COMPLEXITIES OF TREATING OLDER PATIENTS

Older patients are increasingly retaining their natural dentition until later in life and tooth loss remains a reality in the geriatric population. [1,47] The problems regarding treatment of older patients should be carefully evaluated and be part of long-term treatment planning as impaired vision, reduced tactile sensation and other factors related to ageing means that patients are less able to clean their teeth or prosthetic work, particularly implant retained restorations. Medical conditions may play an important factor in decisionmaking, such as the suitability for implants, [41] and there may be problematic oral conditions, such as dry mouth, which make prosthetic rehabilitation and in particular tooth replacement unsuitable. [32] In such cases, the SDA should be considered as atreatment strategy to avoid the undesirable risks and side effects of the insertion of fixedor removable prostheses.

There is an increase in the numbers of studies not supporting the SDA for the period 2007-2014. This includes papers showing increased eating difficulties as the number of occluding teeth reduce, as well as reduced bite force and increased risk TMD. An interesting paper by Shoi *et al.* showed reduced cerebral activity during eating with RPDs rather than teeth due to the oral soft tissues being covered.[48]

The Shortened dental arch continues to be a simplified approach that can maintain adequate function, minimise cost and improve accessibility of the remaining teeth for oral hygiene and augment the prognosis of the remaining teeth. Increased attention has been paid to the Shortened dental arch in recent years and has been widely accepted by the clinicians, patients and healthcare authorities due to increasing elderly dentate population and the ongoing economic changes that affect patients with limited financial resources. There is an increase in the number of publications regarding Shortened dental arch with a trend towards more publications being against the concept. While there is a need for more studies of longer duration and with more specific inclusion criteria, it seems that the Shortened dental arch concept deserves to remain as a treatment option in the absence of evidence against its use.

The demographic of senior adults (i.e., 65 years of age and older) who retained their natural teeth is rising and will be gradually large part of dental practice in the near future [35]. Therefore, to offer care for the partially dentate or edentulous patient, dentist should consider a number of aspects, such as oral functionality, vertical dimension, occlusion, maintenance of hard tissue, and temporo-mandibular joint (TMJ) health, as well as patientcomfort. The functional demands of patients are extremely inconstant and individual, whoare in need of dental treatment to be tailored to the individual's needs and adaptive capability. The World Health Organization (WHO) indicates that a functional, esthetic, natural dentition has at least 20 teeth, while the literature indicates that dental arches comprising the anterior and premolar regions meet the requirements of a functionaldentition. A common partial edentulism scenario is the shortened dental arch (SDA). Thisis a reduced dentition with missing posterior teeth and intact anterior teeth. [40]Such dentalsituation may develop in a considerable number of subjects because molar teeth are

–high-risk teeth‖ and tend to be lost at an earlier stage than anterior and premolar teeth [41,49]. Kayser [40] estimated that the proportion of subjects with SDAs may reach 25% of the population in the age group 41– 45 and it could become 70% in the age group 61–65. SDA has been described as a minimum of four occlusal units which provide functional satisfaction to older adults with sufficient adaptive capacity [40].

Indicates older individuals with a reduced dentition of four intact premolars and one occluding pair of molars have adequate masticatory function and are able to maintain satisfactory levels of occlusal stability. [35,51] The decision to replace missing posterior teeth may depend on various factors including patient's perception of need for the prosthesis and/or diagnosis by the clinician for maintenance of oral health. The traditionalapproach of replacing posterior missing teeth has been with partial removable dental prostheses (PRDPs). Although patients with perceived impaired function have reported benefits from PRDPs, [40] optimal oral hygiene is required to maintain the remaining dentition. [41]

The WHO defines the SDA concept by those patients who are being able to function on 20 occluding units (incisors, canines and premolars in maxilla and mandible) [42]. For many years, it was thought that any missing tooth should be replaced [49], although numerous clinicians and researchers questioned this opinion. Käyser was the first to coin the term ‖shortened dental arch‖ (SDA) to describe the concept of acceptable oral function with partial dentition[50]. Through a number of clinical studies, he and his co- workers concluded that many people could function without a full complement of teeth and that not all missing teeth require replacement[11,44].

With noteworthy advances in material science and the enhancement of clinical techniques, a major challenge in prosthodontics today is not only the creation of dental restorations, but also the successful incorporation of these artificial replacements into a dynamic oral system. It is depicted by demographic data that the relative incidence of the edentulous state is declining. It is believed that the percentage of edentulous persons inthe 75+ age group will decrease by about 50% over the 35-year period from 1990-2025.

However, the absolute number of edentulous and partially edentulous patients is increasing due to a significant increase in this segment of the population. [35] As we move into the new millennium, a new class of partially edentulous patients presents a unique challenge to the treating clinician. The partially dentate patient is less likely to consider a removable partial denture (RPD) as an ideal option for rehabilitation of their dentition. However, financial concerns and other limitations (medical reasons) may render these patients untreatable with current fixed and implant treated modalities.[40] There is controversy regarding the relationship between professionally assessed need and subjective treatment need, especially regarding dental care for elderly patients.[41,42] The traditional approach to restorative dentistry stresses the use of idealized morphological criteria and mechanically oriented concepts. To many practitioners, the preservation of complete dental arches remains the prime aim of restorative dentistry. [49] This morphologically based approach was ironically called the _28 tooth Syndrome' by Levin. [50]An example is the large number of distal extensions RPDs made for patients who donot demand such treatment. Furthermore, too many artificial teeth are often placed on the distal extensions of an RPD, in an attempt to resemble the natural dentition.

The shortened dental arch (SDA) has been described as a minimum of four occlusal units which provide functional satisfaction to older adults with sufficient adaptive capacity. It isa problem-based treatment approach that meets the functional, biological, social and psychological needs of the older adult to an acceptable level and potentially reduces costs of treatment. Evidence indicates older individuals with a reduced dentition of four intact premolars and one occluding pair of molars have adequate masticatory function and are able to maintain satisfactory levels of occlusal stability.[44,50]

# CRITERIA FOR PATIENT SELECTION ACCORDING TO KAYSER [52]

1. Progressive caries and periodontal disease confined to molars.

2. Good long-term prognosis for anterior teeth and premolar.

3. Financial or other limitations of dental care.

## CONTRAINDICATIONS FOR PATIENT SELECTION [53]

4. Patient below age of 50years.

5. Anterior open bite.

6. Severe maxillomandibular discrepancy such as Class II and Class III.

7. Parafunctional habit.

8. Preexisting craniomandibular dysfunction.

9. Marked pathological tooth wear.

10. Marked reduction in alveolar bone support.

## ADVANTAGES OF SDA [47]

11. Simplification of extensive restorative management.

12. Easy maintenance of dentition both for patient and dentist.

13. Simplification of oral hygiene maintenance.

14. Good prognosis for remaining teeth.

## PROGNOSIS OF SDA DEPENDS ON [54]

15. Maintenance of good oral health.

16. Maxillomandibular relation.

17. Age of patient.

18. Periodontal status of anterior and premolar teeth.

# TREATMENT OF DISTAL EXTENSION CASES USINGSDA

- The shortened dental arch (SDA) is ‒a dentition with a reduction of occlusal units starting posteriorly.‖ An occlusal unit means ‒a pair of antagonist teeth that supports the occlusion (e.g., premolars and molars).‖

- According to the SDA concept, all treatment efforts should be concentrated on preserving sound anterior and premolar teeth and avoiding extensive restorative treatment in the molar regions. The occlusion is stabilized and the remaining dentition is rehabilitated without replacement of missing posterior teeth. [54]

- Clinical trials showed that an SDA comprising the anterior and premolar teeth appeared to have, in the long term, sufficient adaptive capacity to ensure adequate oral function in terms of chewing ability, aesthetics, stability of the dentition, temporomandibular joint (TMJ) function, and functional habits. [55] However, in many situations, planning the restorative dental treatment according to the SDA concept is contraindicated. Furthermore, some patients, particularly younger ones, may be reluctant to leave their SDAs unrestored. Also, there are still situations where extending the SDA should be considered, where loss of posterior teeth creates, for example, aesthetic problems, occlusal instability, or chewingdifficulties. When a decision is made to extend the SDA, this can be achieved by either a free-end saddle removable partial denture (FESRPD), cantilevered fixed bridge, or by an implant-supported prosthesis. The decision about what would provide the most acceptable treatment option, functionally and aesthetically, depends on a variety of factors. Clinical experience has shown that each treatment option for SDA patients has, in some respects, unsatisfactory elements.

Furthermore, these options should be approached carefully after thorough assessment and detailed treatment plan. The resultant problems in treatment decision-making in this situation have resulted in it being called –a prosthodontic dilemma.‖ [55] The removable partial denture (RPD) can be considered a popular and simple treatment option for the SDA. However, the extent to which this treatment modality may contribute to oral function in patients with SDAs is notyet clear. It is also not yet clear which SDA cases are most suitable for the restoration by an FESRPD so that a positive outcome is more likely to be achieved. [32]

- The objectives of this paper are to review and summarize the current literature about the outcome of extending the SDA by an FESRPD and also to outline the factors that may affect the prognosis of such prosthetic treatment.

# THE PROBLEM OF FREE-END SADDLE REMOVABLE PARTIAL DENTURE

- Extrapolating the existing literature shows that FESRPDs are problematic. This is because planning of an FESRPD may present the dentist with difficulty in achieving the aim of providing a satisfactory and comfortable denture because of the different and differing responses of teeth and mucosa to occlusal loads and the associated clinical problems relating to support and stability. According to Ritchie, [56] the majority of FESRPDs, especially mandibular dentures, are not worn. The essence of this problem is related to the supporting tissues. In most cases of FESRPDs, denture support tends to be derived mainly from the mucosa covering the edentulous areas. When it is shared by the remaining teeth and associated periodontal membranes plus the mucosa of the saddles, the mixed nature of this support creates difficulty in distributing the masticatory forces in an even way. This is attributable to the difference in the displacement properties between the periodontal membrane and the mucosa; the latter is much more compressible than the periodontal membrane. When occlusal forces are applied to such RPDs *in situ*, uneven displacement of the supporting tissues tends to occur and the denture may rotate around an axis joining the most distal occlusal rests. These rotational forces affect the stability of the RPD and these, in turn, may generate damaging forces that in the long term may affect the abutment teeth and enhance residual ridge resorption. [40]

- The aforementioned problem assumes greater prominence in the mandible where the available area of non-tooth support is significantly more reduced than in the maxilla where the hard palate offers greater distribution of load. As a result, the mandibular FESRPD is considered to result in, relatively speaking, more bone loss in the edentulous saddle areas of the mandible *vis-à-vis* the maxilla, and thereby aggravates the potential for FESRPDs to rotate about the abutment teeth [57]. Table 1 summarizesproblems of FESRPDs.

# TABLE 1

- A list of problems that may be associated with FESRPDs

| Problem | Origin of the problem |
| --- | --- |
| Uneven denture support | • Support is usually derived from the remaining teeth and the mucosa covering the posterior edentulous saddles<br>• There is a difference in displacement properties of the supporting tissues. Mucosa is much more compressible if compared to teeth<br>• The mucosa itself may not be uniform in its thickness and displaceability all over the residual ridge |
| Inadequate denture retention | • Denture bases adjacent to the remaining teeth are directly retained by two clasps but no direct retention elements can be provided to retain the posterior part of the denture base<br>• Though an indirect retention element can resist the rotational movement of the denture base, the effectiveness of indirect retention is far more reduced when the indirect retention element is placed very close to the axis of rotation (for example in extremely SDA cases) |
| Insufficient denture stability | • The potential for poor stability of the free-end saddle of the denture base may be the result of poor support and inadequate direct retention.<br>• In cases with resorbed or flat ridges, denture resistance to lateral and horizontal forces is highly reduced |
| Oral discomfort | • Factors that may induce oral discomfort include: Fragile or resorbed underlying ridge, uneven denture support, inadequate denture retention and/or insufficient denture stability |
| Damage to the supporting tissues | • Abutment teeth may be subjected to torque forces coming from the clasps and aggravated by the rotational movement of the denture base.<br>• Torque forces may be enhanced by the use of inflexible dental clasps or clasps that engage mesial undercuts.<br>• Placement of distal rests on the most posterior abutments may increase the distal torque forces<br>• Resorption of the underlying ridge without concurrent relining of the denture base may exert further damaging torque forces on the abutment teeth which may lead to periodontal destruction.<br>• The continuous friction between the dental clasps and the buccal surface of the abutment teeth coupled with the existence of torque forces may lead to dental abrasion, dental sensitivity and/or dental caries of abutment teeth<br>• Poor support and stability may accelerate ridge resorption and induce tissue inflammation or other oral lesions |

FESRPDs: Free-end saddle removable partial denture, SDA: Shortened dental arch

# CLINICAL INVESTIGATIONS ON THE OUTCOME OFTREATMENT WITH FESRPDS

- Clinical surveys indicated a high failure rate of FESRPDs, especially in the mandible.[69] The ultimate failure may be perceived as the abandonment of wearing the provided dentures for a variety of reasons. Elias and Sheiham indicated that great numbers of FESRPDs are not worn because subjective needs for the replacement of missing teeth in such cases are less than normative needs. This underlines a gap between patients' and dentists' perception of this prostheticrestoration. Furthermore, inadequate quality of prescription in designing RPDs forpatients with SDAs has been reported. [58]

- Kayser *et al.* [59] considered the prosthodontic intervention to extend the SDA by an FESRPD to be a kind of ‒overtreatment.‖ The same authors believed that such treatment does not contribute to the maintenance of a healthy, natural functioning dentition for life. By contrast, the provision of an FESRPD may introduce unfavourable conditions for the remaining dentition.

- Clinical trials by the Nijmegen group questioned the contribution of FESRPDs to oral functions. Their work indicated that extending an SDA consisting of three to five occlusal units by an FESRPD did not lead to an evident improvement in oral function in terms of chewing ability, oral comfort, aesthetics, stability of the dentition, TMJ function, and functional habits.[73] Witter and associates challenged what was a strongly held view for the rationale of providing RPDs. They stated that undertaking conventional removable prosthodontic intervention as a routine preventive measure in SDAs to avoid occlusal collapse should be discouraged. It seems that SDAs comprising the anterior and premolar teeth are able to maintain along-term occlusal stability. Moreover, when molar teeth were replaced by an FESRPD in SDA patients or not replaced in accordance with the SDA concept, nosignificant differences were detected between both treatment modalities in the incidence of tooth loss at 38 months post treatment. This result was confirmedover a 5 years follow-up. [10]

- Leak *et al.* studied the relationship between oral function and the number ofposterior occluding pairs of teeth. The authors concluded that replacement of missing posterior teeth with an RPD would appear to have a small socio- functional impact till the patient has fewer than three posterior functional units.

- Randomized controlled trials showed that extending the SDA by cantilevered fixed resin-bonded bridges offered an effective alternative treatment option to conventional mandibular RPDs at a lower biological price. In a review of the literature, the old dogma of prescribing the RPD on prophylactic ground, that is, to prevent disorder of oral functions, was questioned. The authors indicated that the feasibility to plan the restorative dental care according to the SDA concept should preclude the indication for an RPD. [60] In line with this view, Aras *et al.*

concluded that an SDA with bilaterally missing molar teeth can be an effective alternative to FESRPDs with regard to masticatory performance despite the significant reduction in maximum occlusal force and occlusal contact area. The results of this study demonstrated no significant differences in masticatory performance between SDA subjects wearing FESRPDs and SDA subjects without an FESRPD. In extremely SDAs, rehabilitation with FESRPDs resulted in improved masticatory performance and masticatory time. However, this was not comparable with mastication levels of completely dentate subjects. [10] Creugers *et al.* found that mandibular FESRPDs do not affect temporomandibular function and do not contribute to posterior occlusal support in SDAs comprising three to five occlusal units, with a minimum of one occlusal unit at each side. The authors indicated that such treatment option for the SDAs seems to restore only a fraction of occlusal support in terms of occlusal contacts by these dentures. A similar finding was reported by an earlier study.

- In a recently published systematic review, the authors concluded that the evidence is not yet sufficient to draw conclusions about the relative effectiveness of fixed partial dentures and RPDs in the restoration of the SDAs. [4]

## PATIENTS' ATTITUDES TOWARD FESRPDs

- Jepson *et al.* found that patients' compliance with wearing RPDs was significantly related to the presence of anterior replacement teeth. Dentures that were never worn were more likely to have no replacement anterior teeth. Armellini *et al.* reported similar findings and stated that RPDs had a positive impact on the qualityof life of subjects with SDAs only when the denture replaced anterior teeth. The study of Nassani *et al.* revealed that patients place little value on both acrylic and metal-based RPDs that replaced missing molar teeth in an SDA. Ikebe *et al.*indicated that elderly patients attached higher utility values to cantilevered fixed bridges and metal FESRPDs than to the options of implants and no replacement ofmissing molar teeth for the SDAs. However, the study population in both the aforementioned studies was not SDA subjects and the study design was based on hypothetical clinical scenarios. When patient satisfaction was assessed following restoration of mandibular SDAs in a randomized controlled trial, resin-bonded bridges were considered a more comfortable and acceptable treatment optionwhen compared with bilateral FESRPDs.

- A multicentre randomized clinical trial indicated that restoration of the SDAs withRPDs significantly improved oral health-related quality of life as measured by the Oral Health Impact Profile (OHIP-49) before treatment, and 6 and 12 months after treatment. However, only 10 out of 17 participants who received the RPD treatment completed the 12 months follow-up trial. The provided RPDs were made with conventional cast framework retained by precision attachments. Furthermore, no significant differences in oral health rating were noted between the SDA subjects who were treated by an RPD and the subjects who were treated according to the SDA concept by preservation of a premolar occlusion and non- replacement of molar support. [12]

- It seems that that the prognosis of FESRPD is not predictable and its contribution to oral functions in patients with SDAs is considered to be dubious. The cantilevered fixed resin-bonded bridges can be considered a more efficient and comfortable treatment alternative for patients with SDAs. In some cases, extending the SDA by an FESRPD may have a positive impact on masticatory function, patient satisfaction, and oral health-related quality of life. However, no significant differences in the outcome of treatment were recorded when the SDA was treated according to the SDA concept or by an FESRPD. Moreover, restoration of the SDAs by FESRPDs incurs more costs to deliver and follow-up the treatment when compared with a functionally oriented treatment according to the SDA concept. This is coupled with increased biological price.

- Despite these findings, the FESRPD will probably continue to be a preferable treatment option when a decision is made to extend the SDA. This may beattributable to economic considerations, as such treatment is relatively cheap, simple, non-invasive, and within the skills and experience of most dentists. However, in the long term, the costs of maintenance and repair and the potential for failure should be considered. It could be argued that a study into the cost- effectiveness of RPD treatment for patients with SDAs is required. The questionto be raised at this point is: Which SDA cases are most suitable for the restoration by an FESRPD? To answer this question, there is a need to identify the factors that may be responsible for the success or failure of this treatment. This may lead to a more guided treatment decision.

- Fueki *et al.* found that young age, increased number of missing occlusal units, asymmetric dental arch, and the existence of chewing complaint are considered significant predictors for seeking prosthetic restoration in subjects with SDAs. This study illustrated that seeking prosthetic restoration was encountered in 3% of SDA subjects with missing second molar(s), in 58% of SDA subjects with missingfirst and second molars, and in 93% of SDA subjects with missing premolar(s). The authors concluded that the perceived impairment of chewing ability due to decreased number of occlusal units is a decisive factor for prosthetic restoration ofthe SDAs. Witter and associates reported that extending the SDA by a fixed or a removable prosthesis depends on the degree of the shortening and the patient's perceived impact on oral health-related quality of life. They stated that there is no evidence to support the prosthetic extension of slightly SDAs (i.e., SDAs with missing molar teeth). Moderately SDAs (i.e., SDAs with missing molar and first premolar teeth) can be extended in exceptional cases, particularly for aesthetic reasons. Extremely SDAs (i.e., SDAs with missing molar and premolar teeth) and asymmetrical extremely SDAs should be prosthetically extended. However, the authors indicated that in such cases, restoration of the SDA should be kept to the level of a moderately SDA, which means that using fixed bridges rather than RPDs may be sufficient to achieve this target. Knezović Zlatarić *et al*. examined 205 patients with RPDs. 57.4% of the maxillary dentures were class I Kennedy RPDs and 28.8% were class II Kennedy RPDs. In the mandible, 75.2% of the RPDs were class I Kennedy and 17.1% were class II Kennedy. No impact on patients' evaluation of the quality of their RPDs was related to patient's age,ability of self-supporting lifestyle, social and economic status, marital status,smoking habits, presence of chronic diseases, and the period of use of present RPDs. Also, factors such as Kennedy classification, denture base material, denturebase shape, and denture support did not have significant impact on patients'general satisfaction or comfort of wearing RPDs. However, the outcome of this study revealed that patients with a higher level of education were less satisfied with aesthetics and hygiene of their dentures. Also, less satisfaction with chewing was recorded among males with mandibular RPDs. Furthermore, it was found thatgreater the number of missing teeth in the mandible, lesser was the oral comfort with the mandibular RPD. [2]79

- Based on the current evidence, Table 2 outlines some factors that may affect the outcome of extending the SDA by an RPD. This may be of some help for dental clinicians when managing these cases and a guide for treatment decision making.

## TABLE 2

- Factors that may affect the outcome of extending the SDA by an FESRPD

| Extending the SDA by a FESRPD may lead to a positive outcome | Extending the SDA by a FESRPD may lead to failure |
| --- | --- |
| • The existence of chewing complaint<br>• Patient's desire for tooth replacement<br>• Young age<br>• Presence of anterior replacement teeth<br>• Moderately and extremely SDAs (Increased number of missing occlusal units, less than 3 occlusal units)<br>• Asymmetric SDAs | • Absence of apparent subjective need for tooth replacement (no perceived esthetic or chewing problems)<br>• Patient's negative attitude towards treatment with removable dentures or lack of ability to manage dentures<br>• Slightly SDAs (I.e., SDAs with missing molar teeth)<br>• Mandibular SDAs with poor ridge support |

FESRPDs: Free-end saddle removable partial denture, SDA: Shortened dental arch

# EVOLUTION OF THE MASTICATORY SYSTEM

An overview of the evolution of the mammalian stomatognathic system and its relation to cur- rent concepts in occlusion provide insights into the requirements for harmonious stomatognathic function in human beings The evolution of the vertebrates from filter feeding jawless fish to extant species has taken almost five hundred million years. Evolutionary changes in the head, jaws, and teeth have been critical in  ensuring mammals' advantage.

It has been suggested that it is the evolution of the mammalian jaws and jaw joints, along with changes in ear structure, that is a key to mammalian success. With prolonged intrauterine growth and subsequent suckling, the period of growth when a young animal has to fend for itself is greatly reduced. Hence the need for continual changes and enlargement of a functioning dentition is lessened, and fewer generations of teeth are required. Thus, instead of being polyphyodonty, mammals are mostly diphyodont. [61]

Fossil evidence shows that there was a gradual increase in size of the tooth-bearing surface of the lower jaw, and reduction of the posterior segment. The mandible gradually extended posteriorly until it came into contact with the squamosal portion of the temporal bone where a new jaw joint, the temporomandibular joint, was established. [62]

The tooth form gradually evolved to consist of a series of cusps, initially in the mesial and distal aspects of the crown, but later forming a triangle  of cusps  called  the trigon.The cusps were subsequently added posteriorly to the lower molars to form a heel or a taloned. Thus, primitive cuspal morphology was established.[63]

The discovery of several specimens of a small fossil hominid in the Hadar region of Ethiopia in the 1970s dramatically changed our concepts of the timing and the order of changes of human evolution. It is believed that two branches arose from the early hominids. One of these branches led to the first members of the genus Homo, Homo habilis. The transition from the early hominid, Australopithecus Afarensis, to Homo Habilis has not been well documented by fossil records but appears to have resulted in a gradual evening out of the whole dentition with diminution of its relative size, loss of diastemas mesial to the canines, a more parabolic dental arch, lessening of sub nasal prognathism, and a decrease in the size and prominence of the zygomatic arch. [64]

The Homo line is distinguished by encephalization seen initially in Homo habilis, but much increased in subsequent species. Thus, the relative proportion of cranium to jawshas changed in humans due to both an increase in cranium size and a decrease in jaw size (Fig 1).

The development of cooking methods allowed greater ease of mastication. Having good dentition was no longer necessary for survival and the freeing of human dentition from evolutionary pressure was accentuated, a process that may have started with the acquiring of upright posture and bipedalism.[65]

Dental reduction has been so widespread among human populations to render the phenomenon of reduced tooth size worthy of scientific explanation. One model invoked to explain structural reduction in organisms is referred to as the probable mutation effect.[66]

According to this model, structures no longer functional due to environmental or cultural changes will experience a relaxation of selection pressure, permitting an accumulation of mutations in the population that will inevitably result in a reduction in size or eventual loss of the affected structure.

Opponents of the probable mutation effect theory purpose models of dental reduction based on natural selection which, unlike the earlier theory, is testable in both modern and archaeological populations. [67]

Therefore, the net effect has been a reduction in direct dependence on the stomatognathic system for survival and a resultant alteration in the size and function of dentition. Current concepts of occlusion emphasize the capability of the masticatory system to adapt to or compensate for some deviations within the range of tolerance ofthe system. Normal occlusion implies a situation commonly found in the absence of disease, and normal values in a biological system are given within a variable physiological range. [44] Therefore, normal occlusion should imply more than a range of anatomically accepted values, and should also indicate physiological adaptability and theabsence of pathological manifestations.

The concept of an ideal or optimal occlusion refers both to an esthetic and to a physiological ideal. The emphasis has moved more and more from esthetic and anatomical standards to a current concern with function, health, and comfort that may include patients exhibiting SDA.[68]

Although a concept of ideal occlusion enables a student to understand stomatognathic physiology and occlusal concepts, most patients with functionally sound occlusions anda healthy periodontium will not require invasive treatment to restore their dentition to an ideal.[69]

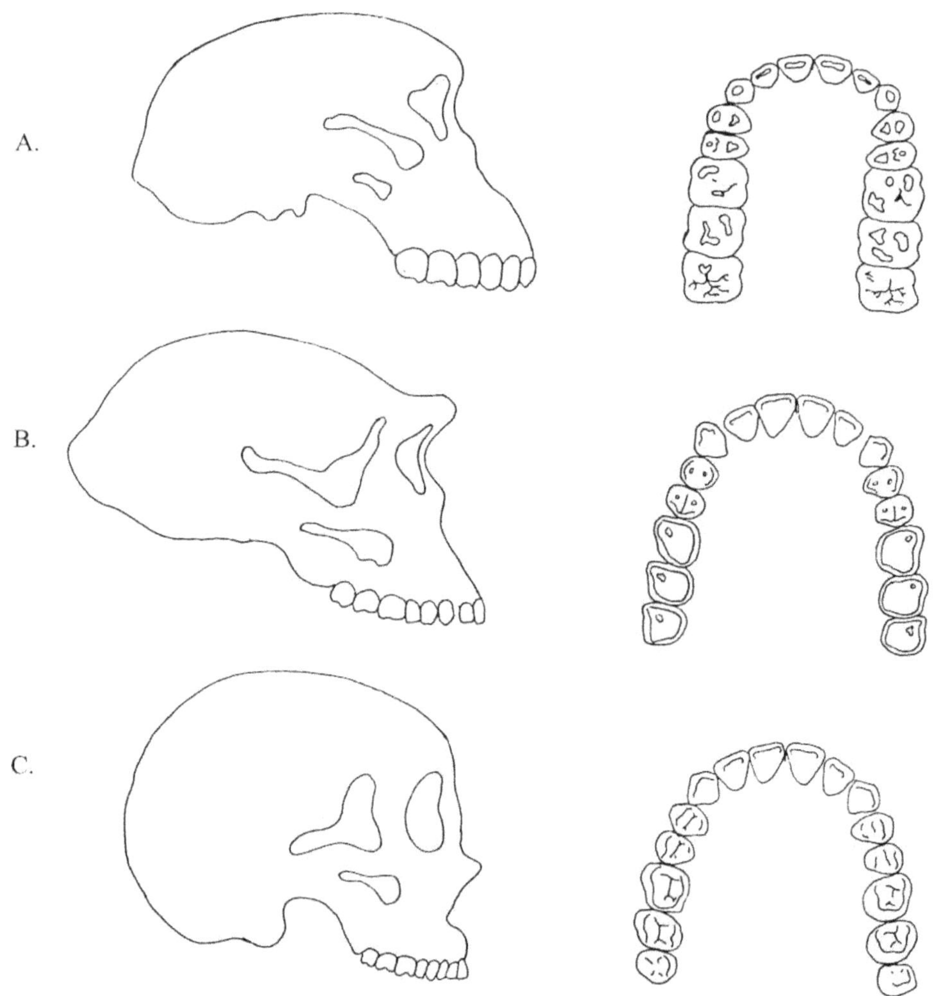

Figure 1. Representation of dental arch diminution with corresponding increases in cranial capacity.

# BASIS OF A SHORTENED DENTAL ARCH CONCEPT

Prosthodontists often approach the treatment of the shortened dental arch as a reconstructive or rehabilitative problem. These terms are introduced to differentiate between rehabilitation procedures aimed at restoring dental and temporomandibular joint function and reconstruction that implies a more anatomically oriented restoration of tooth surfaces. [70] The decision to restore all the teeth in the mouth should be made only after all intended advantages of such treatment are carefully considered and are found to outweigh the benefits of a more limited yet therapeutically sound alternative. [71] The decision should be based on the aim to create and maintain a healthy occlusion. A healthy occlusion as described by Ash and Ramfjord implies an absence of pathology not only on the dentition but also in the periodontal, osseous, and muscular components of the oral system. An orthopedically stable centric position, axial loading of the dentition, and guidance from centric to eccentric positions are also essential. The last requirement is adaptability of the system to changes in other components in the system. [72]

The shortened dental arch concept includes an examination of the dentition within the functional needs of the stomatognathic systems and the requirements of the dentition to maintain a pathology-free system. [73]

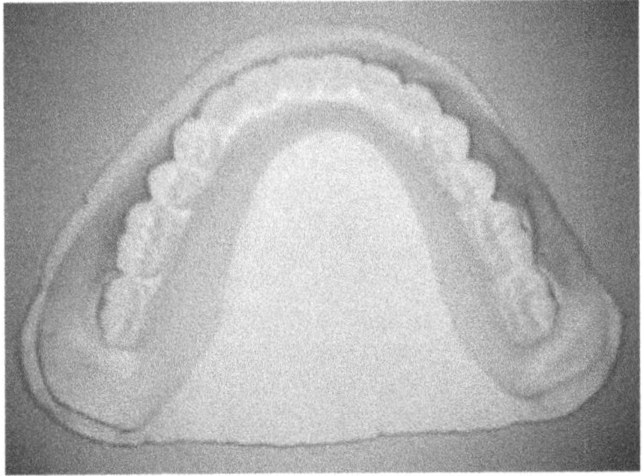

Figure 2. Anatomically complete dental arch.

# THE SHORTENED DENTAL ARCH

A classification for the shortened dental arch, suggested by Kayser,20 groups patients according to the number of teeth remaining in the arch and the symmetry of the shortening (Figs 2–4). [74]

A system considering occlusal units as premolar equivalents was also developed in which a molar is equivalent to two premolar units and a premolar is equivalent to a single occlusal unit. Thus, a single arch of four molars and four premolars would account for 12 occlusal units.

Varying opinions regarding the influence of a shortened dental arch on the masticatory system have been reported. A major objection to the replacement of bilaterally distal edentulous spaces was poor patient acceptance of a traditional removable partial denture; however, the success of implant-borne prostheses has provided a viable alternative treatment modality for the shortened dental arch situation. [75]

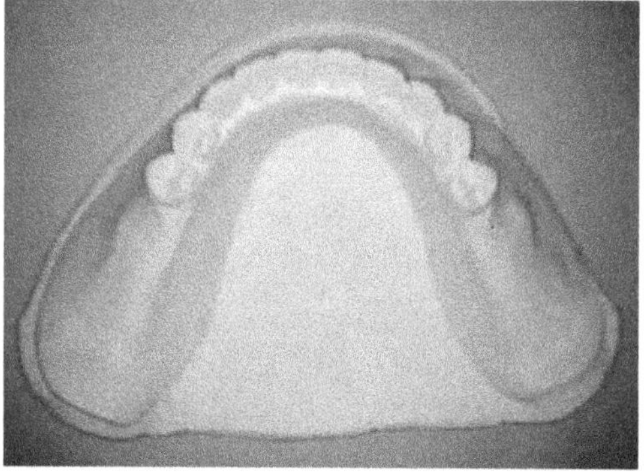

Figure 3. Symmetrically shortened dental arch.

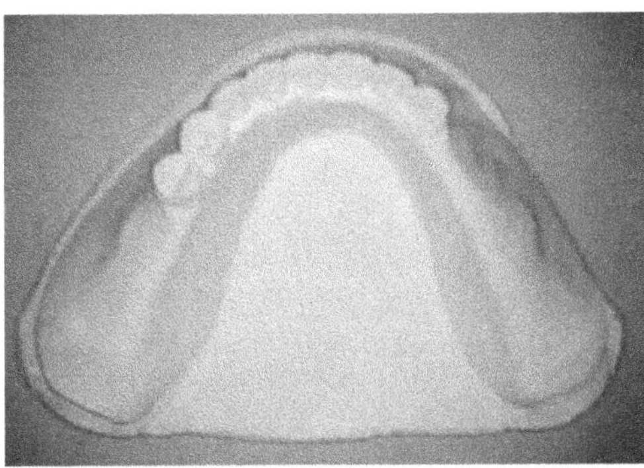

Figure 4. Extremely shortened dental arch with asymmetry

The occlusal preservation target was developed to differentiate the dental arch into strategically important regions. The anterior and premolar regions are functionally and esthetically indispensable throughout life and are considered a priority in rehabilitation. The molar regions play important roles in mastication and stabilization and are usually restored once satisfactory rehabilitation of the anterior segments is completed. In essence, the shortened arch concept allows for treatment and maintenance of strategically important segments before segments of secondary importance are restored.[76]

# SHORTENED DENTAL ARCHES AND ORAL FUNCTION

The functional capabilities of SDA were assessed by chewing tests based on the release of light- absorbing materials when chewing raw carrots. The chewing tests showed a highly significant correlation between masticatory capacity and the number of occlusal units. With a decreasing number of occlusal units, the numbers of chewing strokes needed before swallowing increased. [77]

The subjects started complaining about their masticatory function when the number of occlusal units was less than four in symmetrically shortened arches and less than six in asymmetrically shortened arches.

The preliminary conclusion was that there is sufficient adaptive capacity in SDA when at least four occlusal units are left, preferably in a symmetrical position, and this assumptionhas not been disproved. [78]

## SUBJECTIVE EXPERIENCE OF MASTICATION IN PATIENTS WITH AN SDA

A study was carried out to evaluate the subjective experience of patients masticating with a shortened dental arch. [79]

The aim was to determine whether subjects with an SDA displayed an  increased incidence of chewing problems and whether they had a different food perception and foodselection leading to changes in diet.

A check was made to find out if there were differences in texture judgments, preferences, and actual consumption of 16 different foods between the SDA group and a control group.

On the whole, nosignificant differences were found between the groups. [80]

Other studies have shown that patients may compensate for posterior tooth loss bychewing longer, by swallowing larger food particles, or by selecting a softer diet. [81] Although some investigations have indicated improved chewing efficiency with a distal extension removable partial denture a study by Gunne indicated that no major changes in diet were to be expected.

# AGE AND THE EFFECTS OF THE LOSS OF TEETH ON DIET AND NUTRITION

The practical implications of recognizing different functional levels for individual patients before developing and instituting treatment may be the most significant conceptin the SDA rationale. [82]

One study reported that with appreciable tooth loss there is a related decline in masticatory function, resulting in a compromised nutritional state. However, the theory of prosthodontic re-habilitation improving masticatory function and limiting the risk of severe nutritional problems has not been proven.

Studies have indicated that the distribution of opposing contacts is more important to patients than the relation between missing teeth and function. A study by Smith and Sheiham also showed that only 42% of those clinically assessed as needing treatment felt they required treatment, and only 19% had tried to obtain it. [82]

# MANDIBULAR DYSFUNCTION SYNDROME AND POSTERIOR EDENTULISM

Costen in the year 1935 noted that ear and sinus symptoms manifesting as facial pain were often related to disturbed function of the mandibular joints, thus creating the illusionthat temporomandibular joint disturbances could be adequately treated by dental intervention alone. This led to widespread alteration of occlusal vertical dimension by dentists but not always with benefit to the patient. [83]

Sicher recognized the shortfalls of radical occlusal alteration and protested that there was no anatomical support for this reasoning. Current opinion suggests that the cause of temporo-mandibular joint dysfunction is multifactorial and not solely related to occlusal imperfections.

In most instances the mandible functions as a Class 3 lever in the mid-sagittal plane, the tripodal bracing effect of the condyles, and the teeth being in balance around the bilateral pull of the masticatory muscles. [84] Thus, a wider spread of occlusal forces could, in essence, reinforce this braced position. An examination of the alignment of the major closing muscles will show that the combined vector of forces of the masseteric bellies, themedial pterygoid, and the superficial temporalis exert an anterior superior closing force, which is borne mostly by the bracing of the condyles against the anterior slope of the articular eminence and the interlocking of cusps and vertical overlap of the anterior teeth.

[85] Theoretically, the distance of these teeth from the envelope of closing muscles places much of this closing force on the condylar elements; however, research has shown no increase in the incidence of temporomandibular dysfunction in patients with SDA (Fig 5).[86]

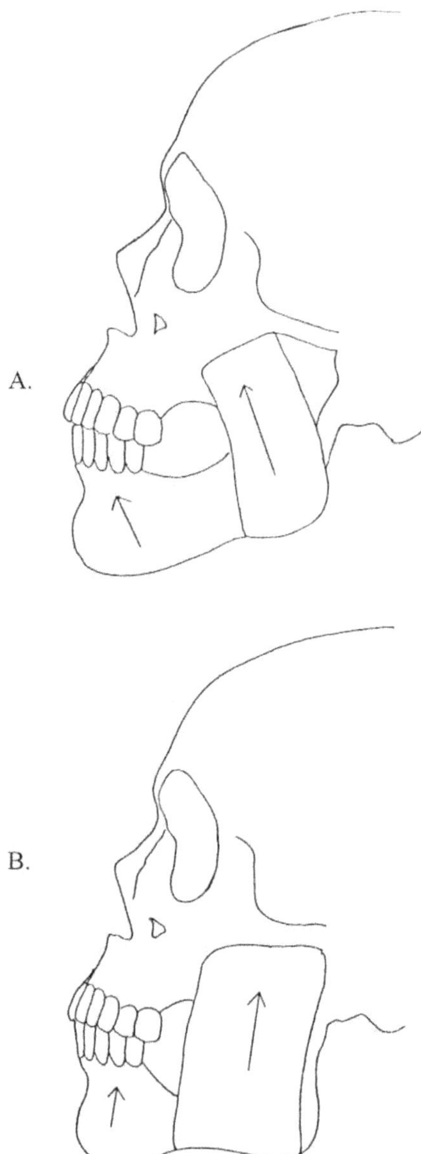

Figure 5. Representation of the lever systems acting on the shortened dental arch. (A) Class II arch relation- ships often result in a significant anterior component to the muscular force. (B) Class III arch relationships result in axial direction of muscular force.

# REVIEW OF LITERATURE

**Kanno T, Carlsson GE (2006)-** The aims of this paper were to review the literature on shortened dental arches with special focus on publications of the Käyser/Nijmegen group,and to evaluate the discussions on the shortened dental arch concept found in the literature. A MEDLINE (PubMed) search was conducted for articles in English published in the dental literature from 1966 to November 2005. The search revealed epidemiological, cross-sectional and longitudinal clinical studies as well as opinion papers, the majority of which were published by the Dutch group. The studies found in general no clinically significant differences between subjects with shortened dental archesof three to five occlusal units and complete dental arches regarding variables such as masticatory ability, signs and symptoms of temporomandibular disorders, migration of remaining teeth, periodontal support, and oral comfort. The findings from cross-sectional studies were corroborated longitudinally. No systematic clinical study with conflicting results was found. The shortened dental arch concept was accepted by a great majority of dentists but not widely practised. The studies reviewed showed that shortened dental arches comprising anterior and premolar teeth in general fulfil the requirements of a functional dentition. It may therefore be concluded that the concept deserves serious consideration in treatment planning for partially edentulous patients. However, with ongoing changes, e.g. in dental health and economy, the concept requires continuing research, evaluation and discussion. Patients' needs and demands vary much and should be individually assessed but the shortened dental arch concept deserves to be included in all treatment planning for partially edentulous patients.

**Abu-Saleh T, Marnewick J (2008)-** The aim of this report is to highlight the efficiencyof implant restoration of a shortened dental arch (SDA) for a partially edentulous patient.

The SDA refers to a dentition with loss of posterior teeth. The goal of dental care is the maintenance of a natural dentition with regard to esthetics, speech, chewing, and oral comfort. In order to achieve this goal several issues were examined in a SDA clinical scenario including masticatory ability, occlusal factors, the effect of removable partial dentures, oral comfort, and periodontal support.A 62-year-old female with a SDA presented for treatment with concern about her compromised periodontal and restorative status. Following professional scaling and root planing and oral hygiene motivation, the bite was opened. Restorative treatment was rendered up to the second premolars with the issues associated with a SDA in mind.A body of evidence in literature showed an arch extending to the second premolars is adequate for normal functional demands, oral hygiene, oral comfort, and possibly reduced costs on a dentition subjected to modern diet.The reported clinical outcomes of using implant supported crowns till the  second premolar area using the concept of restoring only an existing SDA were highly satisfactory for the well-oriented patient.

**De Oliveira BF, Seraidarian PI (2014)-** The purpose of this study was to analyze whether shortened dental arches could result in tooth displacement.Four different 3-dimensional maxillary and mandibular arches with different levels of arch  length reduction were created. In all models, anatomic structures that represent the temporomandibular joint, cortical and cancellous bone, enamel, dentin, and periodontal ligament were modeled. Mechanical properties were attributed to each anatomic component, and a total occlusal load of 100 N on masseter, temporal, and medial pterygoid muscles was simulated for each model. The MSC. Patran software was used for the preprocessing and postprocessing of the biomechanical analysis of the models. One complete dental arch was used as the control.The simulations showed that shortened dental arches presented greater tooth displacements than those found in a complete dental arch. The changes in mandibular tooth position were greater than those observed in the maxillary arches. In finite element models 1 and 2, the largest maxillary displacements were found for posterior teeth.Decreasing numbers of occlusal units resulted in increasingamounts of displacements of the remaining teeth, which may compromise dentalstability in patients with shortened dental arches.

**Wolfart S, Müller F, Gerß J (2014)-** Although the shortened dental arch (SDA) concept is a widely accepted strategy to avoid overtreatment, little is known on its impact on oral health-related quality of life (OHRQoL). This multicenter randomized controlled trial aimed to investigate the OHRQoL for removable partial dental prostheses (RPDP) with molar replacement versus the SDA concept.In both groups, missing anterior teeth were replaced with fixed dental prosthesis. Two hundred fifteen patients with bilateral molar loss in at least one jaw were included. The Oral Health Impact Profile (OHIP-49) was completed before; 6 weeks (baseline), 6 months, and 12 months after treatment; and thereafter annually until 5 years.Of the initial cohort, 81 patients were assigned to the RPDP group and 71 to the SDA group (age, 34 to 86 years). Before treatment, the medianOHIP score was similar in both groups (RPDP, 38.0; SDA, 40.0; n.s.). Results indicate marked improvements in OHRQoL in both groups between pretreatment and baseline (RPDP, 27.0; SDA, 19.0; p ≤ 0.0001) which continued in the RPDP group until the 1-yearfollow-up (p = 0.0002). These significant reductions in OHIP scores are reflected in its subscales. No further differences were seen within and between groups during the remainder observation period. Both treatments show a significant improvement in OHRQoL which continued in the RPDP group until the 1-year follow-up. No significant differences were seen between groups.

**Fueki K, Baba K (2017)-** This systematic review aimed to compare oral health-related quality of life (OHRQoL) between two tooth replacement strategies - the shortened dental arch (SDA) concept and conventional treatment with removable partial dental prosthesis (RPDP) or implant-supported fixed partial dental prosthesis (IFPDP) - for distal extensionof edentulous space in the posterior area. We retrieved eligible randomised controlled trials (RCTs) and non-RCTs published between 1980 and November 2016 retrieved from MEDLINE and the Cochrane Central Register of Controlled Trials. The primary outcome was OHRQoL evaluated using validated questionnaires. Two reviewers independently screened and selected the articles, evaluated the risk of bias and determined the standardised weighted mean difference (SWMD) in OHRQoL scores between the two strategies using a random effects model. Two RCTs and one non-RCT involving 516 participants were included in this review. All studies employed the oral health impact profile (OHIP) for evaluation of OHRQoL. There was no statistically significant difference in OHIP summary scores between SDA and RPDP at 6 (SWMD = 0·24) or 12 (SWMD = 0·40) months post-treatment. Only one non-RCT had reported higher OHRQoL with IFPDP than with SDA; however, because of the small sample size, there was no significant difference in OHIP summary scores between the two strategies at 6 (SWMD = -0·59) or 12 (SWMD = -0·67) months post-treatment. In terms of OHRQoL in partially dentate patients, the SDA concept appears to be as feasible as RPDP restoration. Further clinical trials are required to clarify the effect of IFPDP restoration on OHRQoL.

To compare oral health-related quality of life (OHRQoL) in patients with either molar replacement by partial removable dental prostheses (PRDP) or with restored shortened dental arches (SDA) over a period of 10 years. In this multi-centre RCT, a consecutive sample of 215 patients with bilateral molar loss in at least one jaw was initially recruited in 14 prosthodontic departments. Of those patients, 150 could be randomly allocated to the treatment groups (SDA: n = 71; PRDP: n = 79), received the allocated treatment, and were available for follow-up assessments. OHRQoL was assessed using the 49-item version of the Oral Health Impact Profile (OHIP) before treatment (baseline) and at follow-ups after treatment (4-8 weeks and 6, 12, 24, 36, 48, 60, 96, and 120 months). To investigate the course of OHRQoL over time, we longitudinally modelled treatment and time effects using mixed-effects models. OHRQoL substantially improved from baseline to first follow-up in both groups indicated by a mean decrease in OHIP scores of 20.0 points (95%-CI: 12.5-27.5). When compared to the SDA group, OHRQoL in the PRDP group was not significantly different (-0.6 OHIP points; 95%-CI: -7.1 to 5.9) during the study period when assuming a constant time effect. OHRQoL remained stable over the 10 years with a statistically insignificant time effect (p = 0.848).For patients requesting prosthodontic treatment for their lost molars, treatments with SDA or PRDP improve clinically relevantly OHRQoL and maintain it over a period of 10 years with no option being superior to the other. Since there was no significant difference between the two treatment options over the observation period of 10 years, and since results have stayed stable over time, patients can be informed that both treatment concepts are equivalent concerning OHRQoL.

**AlHmoudi H, Khamis AH (2022)-** This is a cross-sectional study utilizing an online questionnaire anonymously to investigate the awareness and views of dentists about SDA. The questionnaire was sent to all 901 dentists registered with the Emirates Medical Association (EMA). The questionnaire consists of 17 questions, which comprise demographics, awareness, and application in dental practice, preferred treatmentmodality, and risks and benefits associated with SDA. The data were analysed using

SPSS Statistics. The response rate reported was 40.3%. Two-thirds of the respondents (65.8%) were aware of the SDA concept; however, it was not usually applied in clinical practice (n = 196, 54.7%). Specialists were more aware of the concept (p ≤ 0.001) and applied it more frequently in their clinical practice (p=0.041) than general dental practitioners (GDPs). Respondents agreed that SDA was associated with the risks of teeth migration (n = 211, 59.9%), tooth wear (n = 196, 55.8%), and/or temporomandibular disorder (TMD) (n = 163, 45.3%). The implant was the treatment of choice for many of the participants (n = 169, 46.6%) to replace missing molars, followed by the acrylic removal partial denture (RPD) (n = 129, 35.5%). Most dentists who responded to this survey were aware of the SDA concept and had a positive attitude about it. However, theydid not apply it frequently in their clinical practice.

**Agarwal V, Ashok V (2022)-** Oral rehabilitation is essential in patients having multiple missing teeth, to restore aesthetics and function. However, replacement of completedentition may not be possible in high-risk patients or patients of low-income group. The concept of SDA can be utilized in such patients to increase affordability and avoid over restoring. The aim of this study was to understand the prevalence of the requirement of oral rehabilitation according to age and gender of the individual as well as to compare the quality of life of patients rehabilitated with complete and short dental arches. Case sheets of around 28,000 patients were reviewed from March 2019 to June 2020 out of which 113 patients were undergoing oral rehabilitation. To eliminate bias all patients affected by the disease were included in the study. Epidemiological data of the patient along with their ongoing treatment was collected and tabulated in MS Excel sheet. Amongst the patients36 patients were selected using simple stratified sampling and patients were asked to report their quality of life on a VAS scale using a quality-of-life questionnaire. The data was then analysed using IBM SPSS software version 23. The prevalence of oral rehabilitation in males was 53.98% while in females it was 48.02%. Age group of 41-60 years was found to be most commonly undergoing oral rehabilitation. The most common extent of rehabilitation was 2nd molar - 2nd molar, around 23% patients underwent rehabilitation from 1st molar-1st molar and around 10% patients underwent rehabilitation from 2nd premolar-2nd premolar. Patient satisfaction was greatest in patients with complete arch restoration when compared to short dental arch restoration. Amongst SDA restoration patients rehabilitated till the first molar had greater satisfaction than patients rehabilitated till second premolar. With increase in lifespan the need for oral rehabilitationhas increased, however it is not always possible or advised to restore the completedentition of an individual. The present study helps us understand the prevalence of oral rehabilitation according to the gender and age of the patients as well as use of newer concepts such as SDA in the management of high-risk patients. Within the limitations of the present study patient satisfaction was greater in complete arch restoration compared to SDA. Thus, it is important to understand the requirements of the patient and rehabilitate accordingly, so as to provide the patient with the best aesthetics and function possible.

# CONCLUSION

Dentists' attitudes to the SDA concept have shown that the concept is accepted; however, a rational treatment planning sequence for the SDA based on a thorough evaluation of functional, esthetic, and psychological needs is not widely practiced. [32] Much of the opposition to complete restoration of the shortened dental arch has focused on the deficiencies inherently present in removable partial denture prostheses. Quality-of-life assessments have shown that improvements in function are not always associated with the use of removable prostheses. Studies have indicated that as much as 60% of the population of mandibular RPD wearers is dissatisfied with their prostheses. The long- term success of implant-borne prostheses to rehabilitate the partially and completelyedentulous jaw has provided the profession with an alternative to removable prostheses; however, this treatment may not always be possible due to local and systemic factors. [35]

The cost of new technology in dentistry places a primary burden on the patient and a widespread recourse to managed care has placed severe limitations on the number of patients that may be able to avail themselves of the treatment. [40] The question of the shortened dental arch becomes less and less one of effectiveness of treatment and more ofa financial decision.

As prosthodontists, we often spend hours agonizing over minor variables in the execution of treatment. Equally important, as health professionals, it is imperative that we evaluate our patients as individuals, requiring more than just a dentition but a well-functioning, if theoretically incomplete, masticatory system that serves to fulfill each person's varying needs. [87]

# REFERENCES


1.  Käyser AF. Limited treatment goals – shortened dental arches. Periodontology 2000. 1994 Feb;4(1):7–14.

2.  Kanno T, Carlsson GE. A review of the shortened dental arch concept focusing on the work by the Käyser/Nijmegen group. J of Oral Rehabilitation. 2006 Nov; 33(11):850–62.

3.  Leake JL, Hawkins R, Locker D. Social and functional impact of reduced posterior dental units in older adults. J of Oral Rehabilitation. 1994 Jan;21(1):1–10.

4.  Witter DJ, Van Palenstein Helderman WH, Creugers NHJ, Käyser AF. The shortened dental arch concept and its implications for oral health care. Comm Dent Oral Epid. 1999 Aug;27(4):249–58.

5.  Rosenoer LM, Sheiham A. Dental impacts on daily life and stisfaction with teeth in relation to dental status in adults. J of Oral Rehabilitation. 1995 Jul;22(7):469–80.

6.  Teófilo LT, Leles CR. Patients' self-perceived impacts and prosthodontic needs at the time and after tooth loss. Brazilian dental journal. 2007; 18:91–6.

7.  Elias AC, Sheiham A. The relationship between satisfaction with mouth and number, position and condition of teeth: studies in Brazilian adults. J of Oral Rehabilitation. 1999 Jan;26(1):53–71.

8.  Mukatash GN, Al-Rousan M, Al-Sakarna B. Needs and demands of prosthetic treatment among two groups of individuals. Indian Journal of Dental Research.2010;21(4):564–7.

9.  Davenport JC, Basker RM, Heath JR, Ralph JP, Glantz PO. Need and demand for treatment. British Dental Journal. 2000;189(7):364–8.

10. Käyser AF. Shortened dental arches and oral function. J of Oral Rehabilitation. 1981 Sep;8(5):457–62.

11. De Sa E Frias V, Toothaker R, Wright RF. Shortened Dental Arch: A Review of Current Treatment Concepts. Journal of Prosthodontics. 2004 Jun;13(2):104–10.

12. Armellini D, Von Fraunhofer JA. The shortened dental arch: a review of theliterature. The Journal of prosthetic dentistry. 2004;92(6):531–5.

13. Ikebe K, Matsuda K ichi, Kagawa R, Enoki K, Yoshida M, Maeda Y, et al. Association of masticatory performance with age, gender, number of teeth, occlusal force and salivary flow in Japanese older adults: is ageing a risk factor for masticatory dysfunction? Archives of oral biology. 2011;56(10):991–6.

14. Zeng X, Sheiham A, Tsakos G. Relationship between clinical dental status and eating difficulty in an old Chinese population. J of Oral Rehabilitation. 2008 Jan;35(1):37– 44.

15. Krall E, Hayes C, Garcia R. How dentition status and masticatory function affect nutrient intake. The Journal of the American Dental Association. 1998;129(9): 1261–9.

16. Kreulen CM, Witter DJ, Tekamp FA, Slagter AP, Creugers NHJ. Swallowing threshold parameters of subjects with shortened dental arches. Journal of Dentistry. 2012;40(8):639–43.

17. Wayler AH, Chauncey HH. Impact of complete dentures and impaired natural dentition on masticatory performance and food choice in healthy aging men. The Journal of prosthetic dentistry. 1983;49(3):427–33.

18. Fueki K, Yoshida E, Igarashi Y. A structural equation model to investigate theimpact of missing occlusal units on objective masticatory function in patients with shortened dental arches: MASTICATION AND SHORTENED DENTAL ARCH. Journal of Oral Rehabilitation. 2011 Nov;38(11):810–7.

19. Yoshida M, Kikutani T, Yoshikawa M, Tsuga K, Kimura M, Akagawa Y. Correlation between dental and nutritional status in community- dwelling elderly Japanese. Geriatrics Gerontology Int. 2011 Jul;11(3):315–9.

20. Agerberg G, Carlsson GE. Chewing Ability in Relation to Dental and General Health: Analyses of Data Obtained From a Questionnaire. Acta Odontologica Scandinavica. 1981 Jan;39(3):147–53.

21. Sierpinska T, Golebiewska M, Dlugosz JW. The relationship between masticatory efficiency and the state of dentition at patients with non rehabilitated partial lost of teeth. Adv Med Sci. 2006;51(Suppl 1):196–9.

22. Oosterhaven SP, Westert GP, Schaub RMH, Van Der Bilt A. Social and psychologic implications of missing teeth for chewing ability. Comm Dent Oral Epid. 1988 Apr;16(2):79–82.

23. Van der Bilt A, Olthoff LW, Bosman F, Oosterhaven SP. The effect of missing postcanine teeth on chewing performance in man. Archives of oral biology. 1993;38(5):423–9.

24. Battistuzzi P, Käyser A, Kanters N. Partial edentulism, prosthetic treatment and oral function in a Dutch population. J of Oral Rehabilitation. 1987 Nov;14(6):549–55.

25. Montero J, Bravo M, Hernández LA, Dib A. Effect of arch length on the functional well-being of dentate adults. J of Oral Rehabilitation. 2009 May;36(5):338–45.

26. Sarita PTN, Witter DJ, Kreulen CM, Van't Hof MA, Creugers NHJ. Chewing ability of subjects with shortened dental arches. Comm Dent Oral Epid. 2003 Oct;31(5):328–34.

27. Aukes JNSC, Käyser AF, Felling AJA. The subjective experience of mastication in subjects with shortened dental arches. J of Oral Rehabilitation. 1988 Jul;15(4):321–4.

28. Ueno M, Yanagisawa T, Shinada K, Ohara S, Kawaguchi Y. Masticatory ability and functional tooth units in Japanese adults. J of Oral Rehabilitation. 2008 May;35(5):337–44.

29. Wang MQ, Xue F, He JJ, Chen JH, Chen CS, Raustia A. Missing Posterior Teeth andRisk of Temporomandibular Disorders. J Dent Res. 2009 Oct;88(10):942–5.

30. Tallents RH, Macher DJ, Kyrkanides S, Katzberg RW, Moss ME. Prevalence of missing posterior teeth and intraarticular temporomandibular disorders. The Journalof prosthetic dentistry. 2002;87(1):45–50.

31. Witter DJ, Van Elteren P, Käyser AF. Signs and symptoms of mandibular dysfunction in shortened dental arches*. J of Oral Rehabilitation. 1988 Sep;15(5):413–20.

32. Witter DJ, De Haan AFJ, Käyser AF, Van Rossum GMJM. A 6- year follow- up study of oral function in shortened dental arches. Part II: Craniomandibular dysfunction and oral comfort*. J of Oral Rehabilitation. 1994 Jul;21(4):353–66.

33. Hattori Y, Satoh C, Seki S, Watanabe Y, Ogino Y, Watanabe M. Occlusal and TMJ Loads in Subjects with Experimentally Shortened Dental Arches. J Dent Res. 2003 Jul;82(7):532–6.

34. Ishimaru JI, Handa Y, Kurita K, Goss AN. The effect of occlusal loss on normal and pathological temporomandibular joints: an animal study. Journal of Cranio-Maxillofacial Surgery. 1994;22(2):95–102.

35. Witter DJ, Creugers NHJ, Kreulen CM, De Haan AFJ. Occlusal Stability in Shortened Dental Arches. J Dent Res. 2001 Feb;80(2):432–6.

36. Witter DJ, De Haan AFJ, Käyser AF, Van Rossum GMJM. Shortened dental arches and periodontal support*. J of Oral Rehabilitation. 1991 May;18(3):203–12.

37. Douglass CW, Watson AJ. Future needs for fixed and removable partial dentures in the United States. The Journal of prosthetic dentistry. 2002;87(1):9–14.

38. Korduner EK, Söderfeldt B, Kronström M, Nilner K. Attitudes toward the shortened dental arch concept among Swedish general dental practitioners. International Journalof Prosthodontics [Internet]. 2006 [cited 2024 Jan 24];19(2). Available from: https://search.ebscohost.com/login.aspx?direct=true&profile=ehost&scope=site&aut htype=crawler&jrnl=08932174&asa=Y&AN=36852093&h=bSpovLvU8%2Btftv2M oLDcCpe%2FAhY2%2FxU4E8A7y7O3N%2Btio%2FpecdgOB0wqKfsXAQ8LIa% 2FmYXKDOttUl4LaTI6Dlw%3D%3D&crl=c

39. Frank RP, Milgrom P, Leroux BG, Hawkins NR. Treatment outcomes with mandibular removable partial dentures: a population-based study of patient satisfaction. The Journal of prosthetic dentistry. 1998;80(1):36–45.

40. Sarita PT, Kreulen CM, Witter DJ, Van't Hof M, Creugers NH. A study on occlusal stability in shortened dental arches. International Journal of Prosthodontics [Internet]. 2003 [cited 2024 Jan 24];16(4). Available from: https://search.ebscohost.com/login.aspx?direct=true&profile=ehost&scope=site&authtype=crawler&jrnl=08932174&asa=Y&AN=36909219&h=TudF8%2Fb7SJu2%2BsYStyVUSoQa90XvVrMp3KfZm9OA2dutm5NbqGQG2Ap%2B10mbvkNqsKuWw8EhzPcAJN4FJQBPoA%3D%3D&crl=c

41. Lahti S, Suominen- Taipale L, Hausen H. Oral health impacts among adults inFinland: competing effects of age, number of teeth, and removable dentures. European J Oral Sciences. 2008 Jun;116(3):260–6.

42. Yeung ALP, Lo ECM, Chow TW, Clark RKF. Oral health status of patients 5–6 years after placement of cobalt–chromium removable partial dentures. J of Oral Rehabilitation. 2000 Mar;27(3):183–9.

43. Shigli K, Hebbal M, Angadi GS. Attitudes Towards Replacement of Teeth Among Patients at the Institute of Dental Sciences, Belgaum, India. Journal of Dental Education. 2007 Nov;71(11):1467–75.

44. Nassani MZ, Devlin H, Tarakji B, McCord JF. A survey of dentists? practice in the restoration of the shortened dental arch. 2010;

45. Hill J. Report on the shortened dental arch concept. University of Glasglow. 2007;1– 17.

46. Ikebe K, Matsuda K ichi, Kagawa R, Enoki K, Okada T, Yoshida M, et al. Masticatory performance in older subjects with varying degrees of tooth loss. Journalof dentistry. 2012;40(1):71–6.

47. Witter DJ, Allen PF, Wilson NHF, Käyser AF. Dentists'attitudes to the shortened dental arch concept. J of Oral Rehabilitation. 1997 Feb;24(2):143–7.

48. Käyser AF, Battistuzzi PGFCM, Snoek PA, Plasmans PJ, Spanauf AJ. The implementation of a problem- oriented treatment plan. Australian Dental Journal. 1988 Feb;33(1):18–22.

49. Hobdell M, Clarkson J, Petersen PE, Johnson N. Global goals for oral health 2020. International dental journal. 2003;53(5):285–8.

50. Ribeiro MTF, Rosa MAC da, Lima RMN de, Vargas AMD, Haddad JPA, Ferreira e Ferreira E. Edentulism and shortened dental arch in Brazilian elderly from the National Survey of Oral Health 2003. Revista de saude publica. 2011;45:817–23.

51. McKenna G, Allen F, Woods N, O'Mahony D, Cronin M, DaMata C, et al. Cost-effectiveness of tooth replacement strategies for partially dentate elderly: a randomized controlled clinical trial. Comm Dent Oral Epid. 2014 Aug;42(4):366–74.

52. Thomason JM, Moynihan PJ, Steen N, Jepson NJA. Time to Survival for the Restoration of the Shortened Lower Dental Arch. J Dent Res. 2007 Jul;86(7):646–50.

53. Fueki K, Yoshida E, Igarashi Y. A systematic review of prosthetic restoration in patients with shortened dental arches. Japanese Dental Science Review. 2011;47(2):167–74.

54. Fernandes VA, Chitre V. The shortened dental arch concept: A treatment modalityfor the partially dentate patient. The Journal of Indian Prosthodontic Society. 2008;8(3):134–9.

55. Health WEC on RA in O. Recent Advances in Oral Health: Report of a WHO Expert Committee. 1992;

56. Mohl ND. A textbook of occlusion. (No Title) [Internet]. 1988 [cited 2024 Jan 25]; Available from: https://cir.nii.ac.jp/crid/1130282270040296192

57. Witter DJ, Van Elteren P, Käyser AF. Migration of teeth in shortened dental arches. J of Oral Rehabilitation. 1987 Jul;14(4):321–9.

58. Jepson NJA, Allen PF. Short and sticky options in the treatment of the partially dentate patient. British dental journal. 1999;187(12):646–52.

59. Allen PF, Witter DJ, Wilson NH. The role of the shortened dental arch concept in the management of reduced dentitions. British dental journal. 1995;179(9):355–7.

60. Kayser AF. Shortened dental arch: a therapeutic concept in reduced dentitions and certain high-risk groups. The International journal of periodontics & restorative dentistry. 1989;9(6):426–49.

61. Allen PF. Aspects of shortened dental arch therapy. Manchester: The University of Manchester. 1993;

62. Nassani MZ, Devlin H, McCord JF, Kay EJ. The shortened dental arch—an assessment of patients' dental health state utility values. International dental journal. 2005;55(5):307–12.

63. Nassani MZ, Locker D, Elmesallati AA, Devlin H, Mohammadi TM, Hajizamani A, et al. Dental health state utility values associated with tooth loss in two contrasting cultures. J of Oral Rehabilitation. 2009 Aug;36(8):601–9.

64. Nassani MZ, Kay EJ. Tooth loss - an assessment of dental health state utility values: Dental health state utility values. Community Dentistry and Oral Epidemiology. 2011 Feb;39(1):53–60.

65. Käyser AF, Witter DJ, Spanauf AJ. Overtreatment with removable partial dentures in shortened dental arches. Australian Dental Journal. 1987 Jun;32(3):178–82.

66. Allen PF, Witter DF, Wilson NHF, Kayser AF. Shortened dental arch therapy: views of consultants in restorative dentistry in the United Kingdom. J of Oral Rehabilitation. 1996 Jul;23(7):481–5.

67. Devlin H. Replacement of missing molar teeth–a prosthodontic dilemma. British dental journal. 1994;176(1):31–3.

68. Ikebe K, Hazeyama T, Takahashi T, Matsuda KI, Gonda T, Nokubi T. Masticatory performance and prostheses in subjects with shortened dental arches. Nihon Hotetsu Shika Gakkai Zasshi. 2007;51(4):710–6.

69. Picton DCA, Wills DJ. Viscoelastic properties of the periodontal ligament and mucous membrane. The Journal of prosthetic dentistry. 1978;40(3):263–72.

70. Ritchie GM. Partial denture design. 2. Lower free-end saddle dentures. Dental Update. 1982;9(8):429–42.

71. Ritchie GM. Partial denture design. 3. Maxillary free-end saddle dentures. Dental update. 1982;9(9):493–9.

72. Carlsson GE, Hedegård B, Koivumaa KK. Studies in Partial Dental Prosthesis. II An Investigation of Mandibular Partial Dentures with Double Extension Saddles. Acta Odontologica Scandinavica. 1961 Jan;19(2):215–37.

73. Nairn RI. The problem of free-end denture bases. The Journal of Prosthetic Dentistry. 1966;16(3):522–32.

74. Fish SF. Partial dentures. 6. Free-end saddle dentures. British Dental Journal. 1970;128(10):495–502.

75. Ben-Ur Z, Aviv I, Maharshak B. Factors affecting displacement of free-end saddle removable partial dentures. Quintessence International [Internet]. 1991 [cited 2024 Jan 25];22(1). Available from: https://search.ebscohost.com/login.aspx?direct=true& profile=ehost&scope=site&authtype=crawler&jrnl=00336572&asa=Y&AN=386988 44&h=Jv8bXdYoAFZXzQIZEtHXLcpp53MgFZHtnhTJSQSpzAJAmKuAjgyIaA9z okcOtjCeN5aFZntabLE6BugGSkM3Ew%3D%3D&crl=c

76. Neill DJ. The problem of the lower free-end removable partial denture. The Journalof Prosthetic Dentistry. 1958;8(4):623–34.

77. JN A. A clinical survey of partial dentures. Br Dent J. 1952;92:59–67.

78. Anderson JN. The cobaltchromium partial denture. A clinical survey Brit Dent J. 1959; 107:57–62.

79. Tomlin HR. Cobalt-chromium partial denture: A clinical survey. Br Dent J. 1961; 110:307–9.

80. Roberts BW. A survey of chrome-cobalt partial dentures. The New Zealand dental journal. 1978;74(338):203–9.

81. WETHERELL J, RJ S. PARTIAL DENTAL FAILURES: A LONG-TERMCLINICAL SURVEY. 1980 [cited 2024 Jan 25]; Available from: https://pascal-francis.inist.fr/vibad/index.php?action=getRecordDetail&idt=PASCAL8110268070

82. Vanzeveren C, D'Hoore W, Bercy P, Leloup G. Treatment with removable partial dentures: a longitudinal study. Part I. J of Oral Rehabilitation. 2003 May;30(5): 447–58.

83. Nassani MZ, Devlin H, Tarakji B, McCORD JF. Designing cobalt chromium removable partial dentures for patients with shortened dental arches - a pilot survey: DESIGNING COBALT CHROMIUM REMOVABLE PARTIAL DENTURES. Journal of Oral Rehabilitation. 2011 Aug;38(8):608–14.

84. Witter DJ, Van Elteren P, Käyser AF, Van Rossum MJM. The effect of removable partial dentures on the oral function in shortened dental arches*. J of Oral Rehabilitation. 1989 Jan;16(1):27–33.

85. Witter DJ, Van Elteren P, Käyser AF, Van Rossum GMJM. Oral comfort in shortened dental arches*. J of Oral Rehabilitation. 1990 Mar;17(2):137–43.

86. Witter DJ, De Haan AFJ, Käyser AF, Van Rossum GMJM. A 6- year follow- up study of oral function in shortened dental arches. Part I: Occlusal stability. J of Oral Rehabilitation. 1994 Mar;21(2):113–25.

87. Walter MH, Weber A, Marré B, Gitt I, Gerß J, Hannak W, et al. The Randomized Shortened Dental Arch Study: Tooth Loss. J Dent Res. 2010 Aug;89(8):818–22.

www.ingramcontent.com/pod-product-compliance
Lightning Source LLC
Chambersburg PA
CBHW040909130726
48005CB00019BA/3035